T0006043

TARTANS

TARTANS

FROM SCOTTISH CLANS TO CANADIAN PROVINCES

BRENDA RALPH LEWIS

amber
BOOKS

ISBN: 978-1-83886-322-7

Published by
Amber Books Ltd
United House
North Road
London
N7 9DP
United Kingdom
www.amberbooks.co.uk
Instagram: amberbooksltd
Facebook: amberbooks
Twitter: @amberbooks
Pinterest: amberbooksltd

Project Editor: Tom Broder

Printed in China

All pictures courtesy of Amorial Gold Heraldry Services

CONTENTS

Scots Clan Tartans

The roots of the Scots clans stretch back thousands of years to the ancient kingdom of Dalriada. Strong clan loyalties have remained a defining feature of the Scots national consciousness ever since. The clan tartans are one of the most distinctive expressions of this proud and often bloody history.

Over the centuries, the Scots clans suffered much for their loyalty towards national heroes such as Robert the Bruce and their ill-fated royal clan, the Stewarts. The final tragedy, after the failed Jacobite rebellion of 1745, was the attempted break up of the clan system and a ban, lasting some 40 years, on the wearing of the tartan. Yet the clans survived and their tartans were eventually revived in all the brilliant colour and variety shown in this section.

Abercrombie/ Abercromby

• When an Abercrombie laird died, his predecessor's skull was removed from his grave and stored in a niche in church.

• The Abercrombie tartan, first recorded in 1831, has been described as 'Black Watch with white'.

There were two Abercrombie families. The first, the barony of Abercrombie, was established in Fife before 1296 but died out after 1620. In 1636, the title Baronet Abercrombie of Birkenbog, in Banffshire, was granted to Alexander, son of Charles I's grand falconer in Scotland, also called Alexander Abercrombie. The Abercrombies were often mavericks. Some were militant Catholics, against Protestant church reform, while the Abercrombies of Throsk near Stirling, were named in 16th-century records as 'rebels'. One, Thomas Abercrombie of Fife, was charged with murder in 1626.

MODERN ABERCROMBIE TARTAN

Agnew

• In 1426, Andrew Agnew was appointed Constable of Lochnaw Castle.

• Agnews in the USA and Australia descend from a branch who were granted lands at Larne, Ulster by King James VI and I.

The name of the Clan Agnew is believed to originate in the Norman French barony d'Agneauw. The family came to England some time in the late 11th century, after the Norman conquest of 1066. Over the next century, they moved northwards and arrived in the Scots Lowlands some time before 1190. This was when William des Aigneu acted as a witness to a charter between Ranulf de Soulis and the Abbey at Jedburgh. The Agnews of Lochnaw became prominent, serving as hereditary sheriffs of Galloway after 1363. After 1451, they performed the same service in Wigtown.

ANCIENT AGNEW TARTAN

9

Allison

• Patrick Alissone, one of the signatories of the Ragman Rolls of 1296, is a possible ancestor of the Clan Allison.

• The Allison tartan was first seen at John Wight's of Edinburgh in 1882.

Clan Allison originated as a sept of either the Clan MacAlister or of the Clan MacDonald. Tradition has it that the MacAlisters' progenitor was one Alexander MacAlister of Loup, who fought for King Edward I in 1296, during the wars of Scots independence. His English allegiance put MacAlister at risk from his fellow Scots, and to escape their vengeance, he is said to have fled to Avondale in Lanarkshire: once there, MacAlister changed his name to Allison. Another forbear has been named as Peter Alesoun, whose signature appears on a deed that he witnessed at Brechin in 1490.

MODERN ALLISON TARTAN

Anderson

• The Royal Canadian Air Force tartan is an officially registered variant of the Anderson tartan.

• The Anderson tartan is unique in that it has seven colours, and therefore requires a special loom on which to weave it. Other tartans have no more than six colours.

This name comes in two forms – MacAndrew, used in the Highlands, and Anderson, used in the Lowlands. Both, however, have the same meaning, which is 'son of Andrew'. The name can occur in more than one Scots clan, including Clan Ross and Clan Donald. Traditionally, it became associated with the MacDonells of Glengarry, and also with the Glengarry tartan. Mainly, though, MacAndrew/ Anderson is a name that has been linked since the early 15th century as a sept of the association of about 16 families known as Clan Chattan.

ANCIENT ANDERSON TARTAN

WEATHERED ANDERSON TARTAN

Arbuthnott

• The Arbuthnott tartan is based on the design of the Black Watch.

• In 1641, Sir Robert Arbuthnott was created a Viscount and Baron Inverbervie to encourage him to support King Charles I in the English civil wars.

The earliest written form of Arbuthnott was Aberbothenoth, which meant 'mouth of the stream below the great house'. This described a feature on the ancestral estate of Clan Arbuthnott in Kincardineshire. In the 12th century, these lands were acquired by Hugh de Swinton as part of the settlement on the occasion of his marriage to the heiress daughter of Walter Olifard. The first of the family to be described as 'of that Ilk', in 1355, was Philip de Arbuthnott. The Kincardineshire lands have remained in the possession of the Arbuthnotts for more than six centuries.

ANCIENT ARBUTHNOTT TARTAN

Armstrong

• The Armstrong tartan first appeared in *Vestiarium Scoticum* in 1842.

• Clan Armstrong could muster 3000 men for battle at a time.

Traditionally, Clan Armstrong dates from the exploits of a warrior named Fairbairn, who saved the life of a Scots king in battle. Fairbairn's reward was the gift of lands in Liddesdale on the Scots Borders, and a new name: Armstrong, meaning 'strong in the arm.' The first Armstrongs on record were noted in Liddesdale in 1376. It appears, though, that granting them land in the Borders did the local inhabitants no favours. The lawlessness of the Armstrongs became legendary. Among their 'exploits' was the burning of Netherby in 1528 and an attack on Penrith in 1610. Leading members of the family were executed as punishment on both occasions.

ANCIENT ARMSTRONG TARTAN

Baillie

• The Baillie tartan, first recorded in 1819, is a military sett and dates from the time of the Napoleonic wars.

• The Baillie family still hold the barony of Lamington, given to William Baillie in 1368.

The name Baillie comes from an important position, that of baillie or bailiff, a type of magistrate. The name is probably French in origin. An early record appeared in 1311, when William de Baillie served as a juror for a land dispute in Lothian. William Baillie of Hoprig was knighted by King David II in 1357. The Baillie tartan was produced by Wilson's of Bannockburn for the Baillie Fencibles (or 'defensibles,') who were intended to help guard Britain against invasion by Napoleon's forces. The invasion never took place and the Fencibles were disbanded in 1802.

ANCIENT BAILLIE TARTAN

Baird

• The earliest known record of the Clan Baird tartan is dated 1906.

• There was a prophecy, which came true twice, that eagles nesting near Auchmeddan would disappear if the Bairds lost the estate.

Bard, the Gaelic for 'poet', is the origin of the surname Baird. The family became prominent through a valiant deed: the Scots King William I was saved by a Baird when he was threatened by a wild boar. Subsequently, Richard Baird of Meikle and Little Kyp received royal grants of land in Lanarkshire and Robert Baird was awarded the Lanarkshire Barony of Cambusnethan by King Robert the Bruce. This, though, was only the start of Baird eminence. The family became powerful in Aberdeenshire, and George Baird of Auchmeddan married into the family of the Earl Marshal.

ANCIENT BAIRD TARTAN

Barclay

• The Barclay tartan appeared in *Vestiarium Scoticum* in 1842.

• The clan has no 'regular' tartan, but wears the hunting or dress version instead.

The Barclays originated in Normandy and arrived in Scotland in 1067, when Roger de Berchelai and his son John – whose surname meant 'beautiful land' – were among the retinue of Margaret, future queen of King Malcolm III. In reward, the de Berchelais received the lands of Towie from the king. Later, members of the family settled in Urie, Mathers, Gartley and Pierston in Aberdeenshire and Collairnie in Fife. In 1165, Sir Walter de Barkeley was appointed royal chamberlain. Another clan member, Sir David Barclay, supported Robert the Bruce and fought for him in several battles, including Methven, where he was taken prisoner in 1307.

ANCIENT BARCLAY HUNTING TARTAN

MODERN BARCLAY DRESS TARTAN

Bissett

• The Bissett tartan was one of the first to be designed by the Scottish Tartans Society, in 1976.

• After murdering the Earl of Atholl in 1242, William Byset set fire to his house to cover up the crime.

A Norman family called Biset travelled north to Scotland with King William the Lion when he returned from his captivity in England in 1174. The Bissetts, as they soon came to be known, acquired land in Morayshire and soon rose to some eminence. But disaster overtook the family in 1242 after Walter Byset, Lord of Aboyne, lost a joust against his brother-in-law, the Earl of Atholl. Byset was so furious that he then killed his opponent. Walter and his nephew John were forced to flee to Ireland, and in the feud that followed, several Bissetts were murdered.

ANCIENT BISSETT TARTAN

Blair

• The Clan Blair tartan illustrated right, which is based on the ancient Blair tartan design, was approved in 1988.

• Despite their Celtic surname, the Blairs are believed to be Norman in origin.

The Clan Blair was a very ancient Ayrshire family, and received their lands near Irvine as long ago as 1205. The Blairs had a very strong military tradition and fought against the English King Edward I in the 13th century: as a direct result of this defiance, Sir Bryce Blair of Blair was executed by the English at Ayr in 1296. His nephew and heir, Roger de Blair fought for Robert the Bruce and took part in the battle of Bannockburn in 1314. The Blairs increased their power and influence through advantageous marriages that connected them to the Kennedy, Montgomery and Cochrane families.

BLAIR TARTAN

Borthwick

• Mary, Queen of Scots and her third husband, Earl Bothwell, sheltered in Borthwick Castle after their controversial marriage in 1567.

• In 1425, a Borthwick Lord served as a hostage in England as part of the ransom for the imprisoned Scots King James I.

The lands they owned near Borthwick Water in Roxburghshire provided the Clan Borthwick with their family name. The name was Celtic, and very ancient. It is possible that the forbears of the Borthwicks came to Britain with the Roman invasion of 43AD. A later ancestor, one Andreas, accompanied the Saxon Edgar the Atheling and his sister Margaret to Scotland in 1067. In about 1410, Sir William Borthwick acquired lands in the Borders and Midlothian, and not long afterwards members of the family became Lords in Parliament.

MODERN BORTHWICK TARTAN

Bowie

• The Bowie clan tartan was only first recorded in the 1970s.

• Jerome Bowie was King James VI's master of the royal wine cellar between 1585 and 1589.

The Gaelic *buidhe*, meaning fair or yellow haired, may have given rise to the names Bowie and Boyd. Likewise, the Argyllshire name McIlbowie – Bowie for short – might have come from *Macghille Buidhe*, meaning 'son of the fair-haired lady'. Possibly, the Bowies were cattle farmers or herdsmen, since the old term for cattle was *bow*.

The Bowies inhabited Strathspey, where they were followers of Clan Grant. Elsewhere in Scotland, they attached themselves to the MacDonalds. In 1489, John Bowey rebelled against the new King James IV and held out against his army in Dunbarton Castle. Fortunately for Bowey, the King pardoned him.

ANCIENT BOWIE TARTAN

Boyd

• The Boyd tartan, based on the Hay and Stuart of Bute designs, was originally devised for Lord Kilmarnock in 1956.

• The Lordship of Boyd was created in 1454 and Thomas Boyd became Earl of Arran in 1467.

The Boyd family came from Brittany in northwest France, where they were hereditary stewards of Dol. The surname, said to come from the Gaelic *buidhe* meaning 'yellow' or 'fair', may have been a reference to the fair-haired Robert, the 1st High Steward of Scotland. The Boyds were already well established in Scotland by 1205 and were granted lands in Ayrshire after 1263. They were strong supporters of Robert the Bruce. One of the Boyd family, Duncan Boyd, was executed in 1306. Another member, Sir Robert Boyd, fought for Robert the Bruce at the battle of Bannockburn in 1314.

MODERN BOYD TARTAN

21

Brodie

• The earliest known date for the Brodie clan tartan is 1850.

• The tartan was among several uncovered by army clothier George Hunter prior to 1822.

Brodie is one of the oldest of all Scots clan names. Possession of the Brodie lands in Moray was confirmed in the 12th century and, in around 1312, Robert the Bruce gave Michael, Thane of Brodie, a charter. This was the first of many charters that affirmed ownership of land in this part of Scotland. Alexander Brodie of Brodie, who was born in 1617, served as a member of Parliament for Elgin county after 1643. The Lord Protector, Oliver Cromwell, thought highly of Brodie and asked him to negotiate a formal union between Scotland and England. Brodie declined to involve himself in a move that might prove illegal if the Stewart monarchy were ever to regain the English throne. It was a wise decision: King Charles II returned to reclaim his crown in 1660 and appointed Alexander Brodie a judge.

ANCIENT BRODIE HUNTING TARTAN

MODERN BRODIE TARTAN

Bruce

• The Bruce clan tartan dates from 1571, but first appeared in the *Vestiarium Scoticum* of 1842.

• Two other designs, the Old Bruce (now McColl) and the New Bruce (now Grant), were being sold in shops around the turn of the 19th century.

The Bruce surname came from Brix in Normandy. Sir Robert de Brus, who gained lands in Yorkshire for his part in the 1066 conquest, was the progenitor of the Bruce clan. His link with Scotland began in 1124 when his son (also Robert) was awarded the Lordship of Annandale by the future Scots king David I. When war broke out between England and Scotland, the second Sir Robert fought on the English side. Yet, the Scots connection survived and became significant when Robert Bruce, 4th Lord of Annandale married a niece of King William the Lion. This formed the basis for the family's later claim to the Scots throne. Their descendant Robert the Bruce, who achieved the crown in 1306 and Scots independence eight years later, was the 7th Lord of Annandale.

ANCIENT BRUCE TARTAN

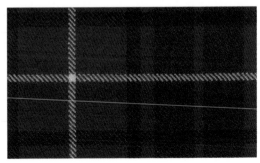

MODERN BRUCE TARTAN

Buccleuch

• The Buccleuch tartan was designed in 1908 and was intended to be worn by the pipers of the 4th Battalion, the King's Own Scottish Borderers.

• A second, 'fancy' Buccleuch tartan was first recorded in the 1830s.

The ancestor of the Scotts of Buccleuch, a sept of Clan Scott, was Richard, grandson of the 12th-century Utredus filius (son of) Scott. Richard's descendant, Robert Scott, inherited the Buccleuch and Murdochston estates during the 14th century. Later, the Buccleuchs acquired a Lordship (1606), an earldom (1619) and a dukedom (1663). The first Duke of Buccleuch was James, Duke of Monmouth, natural son of King Charles II. He married Anne, the Countess of Buccleuch in her own right. He was executed in 1685 after trying to seize the throne.

BUCCLEUCH TARTAN

Buchan

• The Cumming tartan was adopted by Clan Buchan in 1965 to mark the long association between themselves and the Comyns or Cummings.

• The Buchans have been identified as the old 'Tribe of the Land' of ancient Pictish Scotland.

ANCIENT BUCHAN TARTAN

The Buchan-Cumming association began in the 13th century, after the ancient Celtic Earldom of Buchan passed to the Comyn or Cumming family. Shortly afterwards, the Buchans acquired the lands of Auchmacoy in Aberdeenshire and later became staunch supporters of the beleaguered royal Stewarts. In 1689, General Thomas Buchan was made commander-in-chief of Jacobite forces in Scotland by the deposed King James VII (of Scotland) and II (of England and Ireland). James failed to regain his throne, but Buchan fought for James' son, the 'Old Pretender' in the Jacobite rebellion of 1715. Clan Buchan has produced a number of notable personalities, including John Buchan, Baron Tweedsmuir, who wrote the perenially popular adventure story *The Thirty-Nine Steps*.

WEATHERED BUCHAN TARTAN

Buchanan

• The original Buchanan tartan had a symmetrical design, changed to assymetrical around 1831 but restored in 1950.

• The main Buchanan line died out in 1762, when a Buchanan of the cadet branch of Spittal, succeeded as clan chief.

In 1016, Anselan O'Kyan, prince of Ulster, landed in Argyll to fight the Danish invaders. The Scots King Malcolm II rewarded him with the lands of Buchanan, east of Loch Lomond. These lands remained in the family until 1682, when they were sold on the death of John, the 22nd Laird in 1682 when they were sold. The Buchanans were such fierce enemies of the English that after the victory of King Henry V of England at Agincourt in 1415, they joined the 7000 Scots troops who aided Henry's opponent, the French monarch, Charles VI.

ANCIENT BUCHANAN TARTAN

WEATHERED BUCHANAN TARTAN

Burnett

• Anglo-Saxon and also Norman ancestry has been claimed for the Clan Burnett.

• The Horn of Leys, a gift given to the Burnetts by Robert the Bruce, later became the property of the National Trust for Scotland.

The name Burnett is probably a variant of the Anglo-Saxon surname Burnard. However, the Burnetts also claim ancestry from a 14th-century knight of Norman descent, Robertius de Burneville. The Burnards, or Burnevilles, were in the retinue of Matilda of Huntingdon when she came to Scotland to marry King David I in 1113. Soon known as Burnett, the family settled in the Borders. Strong adherents of Robert the Bruce, their loyalty was rewarded with the Forest of Drum, the barony of Tulliboy and, as a symbol of the barony, the jewel-encrusted Horn of Leys.

MODERN BURNETT TARTAN

Burns

• The tartan pictured, right, was produced in 1991 for the Robert Burns Monument at Troon.

• There are five other Burns tartans, one a family tartan dated around 1930-1950, and four versions of an American Burns tartan.

The Burns clan, whose most famous member is poet Robert Burns, probably derive their name from the Anglo-Saxon word *burna*, meaning 'brook'. Burns could also be a shortened version of Burnhouse, a name that connects the clan with the Campbells. Walter Campbell of Taynuilt in Argyll, owned the Burnhouse lands in the 17th century, although his activities during the civil wars caused him to be deprived of his estates and obliged him to go into hiding in Kincaidshire: to help ensure he went undiscovered, it seems that Walter Campbell changed his name to 'Burnhouse'.

BURNS CHECKERED TARTAN

Cameron

• First approved by the clan chief in 1956, the Cameron clan tartan may have derived from the MacFie tartan.

• The name of the Highland Camerons apparently comes from the Gaelic cam-shron, meaning 'crooked nose' or 'crooked hill'.

The ancient Clan Cameron had a warlike reputation. Camerons fought for the Stuart monarchy during the civil wars of 1642–48, although they later became divided over support for King James VII (of Scotland) and II (of England and Ireland). Led by their chief, Ewen of Locheil, Camerons fought on both sides at the battle of Killiekrankie. In 1746, Ewen's grandson Donald fought for King James' grandson, the Young Pretender 'Bonnie Prince Charlie', at Culloden, the battle that finally ended Stuart hopes of regaining the English throne. Wounded, Donald of Locheil managed to escape to France, where he died in 1748. The Cameron estates, meanwhile, were confiscated, but they were eventually restored to the family.

MODERN CAMERON TARTAN

ANCIENT CAMERON HUNTING TARTAN

29

Cameron of Erracht

• Mrs Cameron, designer of the Erracht military tartan, combined Cameron and MacDonald tartans, since the regiment was recruited from both clans.

• The Erracht tartan is the only tartan in the British Army not based on the Black Watch design.

Cameron of Erracht was founded in the 16th century by Ewen Cameron, son of Ewen, Chief of Clan Cameron and his wife, Marjory Mackintosh. The Jacobite rebellion of 1745 saw the Erracht Camerons support Bonnie Prince Charlie. The Erracht tartan is military, and was worn by the 79th regiment, founded by Alan Cameron in 1793. A later name, Queen's Own Cameron Highlanders, was adopted in 1873 to honour Queen Victoria. Tradition has it that the tartan was designed by Alan Cameron's mother. The Cameron clan name was first connected to the lands of Lochiel in 1528, when the territory owned by the 'Captain of Clan Cameron' was converted into a barony by King James V. The Cameron of Locheil is the oldest of the Cameron tartans.

ANCIENT CAMERON OF ERRACHT TARTAN

WEATHERED CAMERON OF ERRACHT TARTAN

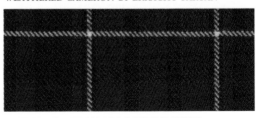

MODERN CAMERON OF LOCHIEL TARTAN

Campbell

• The first mention of the Clan Campbell tartan was in 1725, but it may have been worn much earlier.

• The Campbell of Argyll tartan was based on the design of the Black Watch tartan.

Known as the 'race of Diarmid', the Campbells exerted great influence over Argyll and western Scotland. This began with Colin Mor whose grandson acquired land in Argyll at a time when the MacDougalls dominated. As MacDougall power faded, the Campbell star ascended. In 1457, they achieved nobility when Colin Campbell was created Earl of Argyll by Scots King James II. Two Campbells, however, fell foul of royal authority. Archibald Campbell, the 8th Earl of Argyll, was executed in 1661 for attempting to establish Presbyterianism in Scotland. His son was beheaded for his support of James, Duke of Monmouth, natural son of King Charles II, who attempted to seize the crown in 1685. Despite these setbacks, Campbell power survived and in 1701, Archibald, the 10th Earl was made Duke of Argyll.

ANCIENT CAMPBELL TARTAN

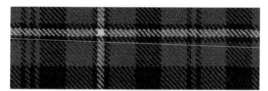

ANCIENT CAMPBELL OF ARGYLL TARTAN

WEATHERED CAMPBELL OF ARGYLL TARTAN

Campbell of Breadalbane

• Part of the regimental uniform worn by a Major Campbell after 1793, in the Napoleonic wars, was used to recreate a version of the Campbell of Breadalbane tartan.

• Campbell of Breadalbane ranked second in importance in the clan, after the Argyll Campbells.

The Breadalbane branch of the Campbells began with 'Black' Colin of Lochawe, who inherited the lands of Glenorchy from his father, Sir Duncan Campbell, in the 15th century. One descendant was Sir John Campbell, 11th of Glenorchy, who became Earl of Breadalbane in 1681. Described as 'cunning as a fox, wise as a serpent and slippery as an eel', Sir John persuaded the Highland clans to support King William III after William's father in law, King James VII (of Scotland) and II (of England and Ireland), was deposed in 1688.

MODERN CAMPBELL OF BREADALBANE TARTAN

Carmichael

• The first known sample of the Carmichael tartan was given to the Highland Society in 1907.

• Clan Carmichael is associated with the Stewarts of Appin and the MacDougalls.

The lands of Carmichael in upper Lanarkshire were originally part of the area granted to the Clan Douglas by Robert the Bruce in 1321. They were transferred from William, Earl of Douglas to Sir John de Carmychell by 1384 and by 1414 had become a barony. The Carmichaels gained their warrior reputation mainly while fighting for the French against the English. The broken spear on the Carmichael crest recalls a dramatic incident at the battle of Beauge in 1421: Sir John de Carmichael shattered his spear when he threw Thomas, Duke of Clarence, brother of the English King Henry V, off his horse.

ANCIENT CARMICHAEL TARTAN

33

Carnegie

• This Carnegie tartan is a variant of the MacDonnell of Glengarry tartan.

• It has been claimed that the Carnegies were cupbearers to the Scots kings.

The Carnegies were descended from one John de Balinhard, who owned lands in Angus. These were sold in the 14th century to pay for another Angus estate: Carrynegy or Carnegie. In 1401, the Carnegie holdings were expanded by John's younger son Duthac when he acquired the lands of Kinnaird through marriage. The Carnegies were staunch supporters of the Scots monarchy. They fought for the Scots kings at the battle of Harlaw in 1411, at Flodden in 1513 and in the first Jacobite rebellion of 1715, after which the Earl of Southesk – a Carnegie title since 1633 – was punished by the forfeiture of his estates.

MODERN CARNEGIE TARTAN

Chattan

• The earliest date for this Clan Chattan chief's tartan is 1816, and it was first recorded in 1831.

• The Chattan tartan, which was also worn by the chief's immediate family, was called 'Finzean's fancy' after the village in Aberdeenshire, where the pattern is still woven.

Clan Chattan – the 'Clan of the Cats' – was an ancient confederation, which grew as further clans sought its protection. Forming its nucleus were the original Chattan federation – the MacPhersons, Cattanachs, MacBeans and MacPhails – and the Mackintosh family with their cadet branches – the Shaws, Farquharsons, Ritchies, McCombies and MacThomases. Other members were unrelated, including the MacGillivrays, Davidsons, Macleans of Dochgarroch, MacQueens of Pollochaig, MacIntyres of Badenoch and the MacAndrews.

ANCIENT CHATTAN TARTAN

Chisholm

• The Chisholm clan tartan, whose design was based on the Black Watch, was first recorded in 1842.

• Mary Chisholm appeared in a portrait wearing the oldest known Chisholm tartan in around 1800.

Both Celtic and Norman ancestry have been claimed for Clan Chisholm, their putative Norman forbears settling in the Borders after 1066. The clan name appears in old records, notably the Ragman Rolls of 1296, in which two early members swear alliegance to Edward I. Later Chisholms were less loyal, fighting for James, the Old Pretender, and his son, 'Bonnie Prince Charlie'. After the defeat at Culloden in 1746, the Chisholms sheltered the Prince from the English. The Chisholm line was among the longest-lasting of all Scots clans. It continued for more than 900 years after the Normans, ending only when the last Chisholm died in the Boer War (1899–1902) in South Africa.

MODERN CHISHOLM TARTAN

WEATHERED CHISHOLM TARTAN

Christie

• Clan Christie were followers of the Clan Farquharson.

• The Christie name was popular in Fifeshire and Stirlingshire in the 15th century.

Christie may be a diminutive of Christian or Christopher. Alternatively, it may derive from Norse Viking, the word 'trusty' or 'thrust' meaning a swordsman. The name was spelled in various ways before settling into its present form. For instance, John Chrysty was a burgess of Newburgh in 1457. A century later, Sir Robert Criste witnessed a deed, and in 1590 Jhone Cristie was a St. Andrews water carrier. A later member of the clan had a glittering career: Thomas Christie, born in 1773 in Carnwath, Lanarkshire, introduced vaccination against smallpox in Ceylon and was physician extraordinary to the Prince Regent, late King George IV.

MODERN CHRISTIE TARTAN

Clark

• The Clark family tartan (illustrated) was first recorded in 1847, and has been variously named as Clerk, Clergy or Priest tartan.

• The muted tones of the Clark tartan accorded with Victorian ideas of what was proper for clergy to wear.

The Clan Clark most probably had origins in the Church, since the name comes from the Latin clericus, meaning 'clerk' or 'cleric'. The Clarks became linked to the Cameron, MacPherson and MacKintosh clans, and many appear to have followed ecclesiastical careers. Not all the Clarks were destined for the church, however. One clan member, Richard Clark, was a vice admiral in the Swedish navy in 1623 and another, George Rogers Clark, emigrated to America in the late 18th century and became a pioneer settler north of the Ohio River.

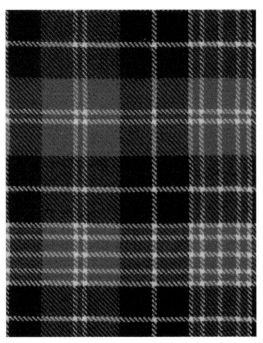

ANCIENT CLARK TARTAN

Cochrane

• The Cochrane tartan lacked its proper red stripe between 1974 and 1984.

• A fragment of the design, which was based on a Lochaber district tartan, was discovered in the foundations of a house in Perthshire.

The Clan Cochrane ancestry may be Viking, dating from before the 10th century, when a Norse invader settled in Renfrewshire. Alternatively, the earliest Cochranes may have come to Scotland some 200 years later; the family are said to have had connections in Renfrewshire 'upwards of 500 years' before Lord Cochrane purchased the lordship and barony of Paisley in 1653. At this time, the eminence of Clan Cochrane was fairly new: it began in around 1638, when William Cochrane acquired the lands of Dundonald, and in 1669 he became the 1st Earl of Dundonald.

MODERN COCHRANE TARTAN

Cockburn

• In around 1816, Sir William Cockburn wrongly identified as his clan's tartan a Mackenzie design worn by the 71st Highland Light Infantry.

• The name Cockburn may have come from Cukoueburn or Cuckoo-burn, a brook on the Scots Borders.

The clan first appeared in the in 1296, when Peres de Cockburne signed the Ragman Rolls. Soon afterwards, the heiress of Sir William de Vipont, owner of the Langton territory in Berwickshire, married Sir Alexander de Cockburn. De Vipont died at Bannockburn in 1314 and his lands became Cockburn family property. Another Sir Alexander de Cockburn, the son of the first, was created hereditary Great Usher after 1373. However, he was imprisoned for a day for brawling with the Earl of Wigtown, who tried to usurp this position.

MODERN COCKBURN TARTAN

Colquhoun

ANCIENT COLQUHOUN TARTAN

• The Colquhoun tartan appeared in the earliest collections of tartans, from 1810.

• Tradition has it that the Colquhouns were official custodians of the crozier once carried by the 6th century Scots bishop St. Mackessog.

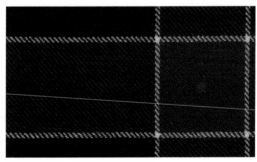

MODERN COLQUHOUN TARTAN

The Colquhoun name comes from Dunbartonshire, where lands were granted to Humphrey of Kirkpatrick by Malcolm, Earl of Lennox in the early 13th century. The Culquohouns, however, had a treacherous history. In 1602, they plotted to trap the MacGregors in Glenfruin, but things went badly wrong: in the bloody conflict that ensued, their chief was killed. In revenge, the Colquhouns persuaded King James VI of Scotland to proscribe the MacGregors and ban the name. The MacGregor clan remained outlaws until 1775.

Cooper

• The Clan Cooper has never had an officially designated chief.

• The pattern of the Cooper clan tartan was taken from a century-old shawl.

Cupar in Fifeshire, once the seat of the ancient thanes of Fife, is one origin of the territorial name Cooper. Another possible source is the cooper's trade itself, which was the making of barrel. The name first appeared in a charter of 1245. In 1281, one John Cupar held lands in Aberdeen, and the same or another John Cupar signed the Ragman Rolls in 1296. During the 17th century, a family named Couper was in possession of the lands of Gogar near Edinburgh, and in 1638 John Couper was made a baronet of Nova Scotia. Two years later, during the Bishops' wars, he was killed in an explosion at Douglas Castle.

MODERN COOPER TARTAN

Craig

• The name Craig or Cragg means 'dweller by the steep or rugged rocks'.

• The Craig tartan, unconnected to a particular clan, was designed for those bearing the surname.

Many Craigs were noted lawyers. Sir Thomas Craig of Riccarton, who was born around 1538, was a famous expert on feudal law in Scotland: his Jus Feudale (Feudal Law) is still used as a reference work by Scots lawyers today.

A branch of the Craig family settled in Ireland after 1610, when the English were establishing plantations in Ulster. The Irish Craigs rose to great eminence. One of them, James Craig, became the first Prime Minister of Ulster in 1921 and was later made a peer, with the title Viscount Craigavon. The new town of Craigavon in County Armagh was named after him.

ANCIENT CRAIG TARTAN

Cranston/ Cranstouns

• William de Cranston was among the guarantors of a truce between England and Scotland in 1451.

• It was said that the Cranstouns invariably lived up to their impudent and selfish motto, 'Thou shalt want before I want.'

Clan Cranstoun derived from the barony of Cranstoun in Midlothian, and also owned territory in Edinburgh and Roxburghshire. In about 1170, Elfric de Cranston witnessed a charter of King William the Lion: Elfric was the first Cranston to be so mentioned. Later on, though, the clan acquired a reputation for banditry. Cranstons frequently took part in raids across the border into England. At some point in the 16th century, the spelling of the family name was changed to Cranstoun, so it was William Cranstoun of Morristoun who was ennobled as Lord Cranstoun in 1609.

MODERN CRANSTON TARTAN

Crawford

• There was no Crawford tartan before 1739, but one was designed between then and 1842.

• In about 1179, Galfridus de Crawford was the first to rule the barony of Crawford in Clydesdale.

Although the family probably came from Normandy or Brittany, the name Craufuird or Crawford comes from two Gaelic words, *crodh phorts*, meaning 'meeting place'. It was appropriate. In the 8th century, the Crawfords were responsible for organizing the place where the chief made policy decisions for his clan. The *Crod phort* was also the origin of the formal 'court' that surrounded chiefs and monarchs. The Crawfords of Auchinames, who became 'chiefs of the name', received a grant of lands from King Robert the Bruce in around 1320, and from then on, the male line remained unbroken until 1879.

ANCIENT CRAWFORD TARTAN

Cumming

• **The Cumming tartan bears resemblances to other clan tartans including the MacPherson.**

• **The Cumming hunting tartan formed the basis of the Gordonstoun school tartan, where the Duke of Edinburgh and King Charles III were educated.**

Clan Cumming (Comyn) has traditionally been traced to one Robert of Comines, in northern France, who came to England with the invasion force of 1066. The Comyns appeared in Scotland after William Comyn was appointed Chancellor by King David I. Comyn power in Scotland grew and Comyns would eventually lay claim to the Scots crown. In this they were thwarted by Robert the Bruce, losing land and titles after he established Scots independence from England. Yet, still the clan flourished in northeast Scotland. In time, the Comyns/Cummings of Altyre became the most prominent part of the family. In the 19th century, Alexander Cumming of Altyre became heir to Gordon of Gordonstown and afterwards assumed both the Gordon name and its arms.

MODERN CUMMING TARTAN

MODERN CUMMING HUNTING TARTAN

Cunningham

• The Cunningham tartan illustrated is known as a 'counter change' because one half of the pattern is a negative reproduction of the other.

• The 1st Earl of Glencairn was killed at Sauchiburn in the same year he received his title.

The name Cunningham, derived from the district of Cunninghame in Ayrshire, was first recorded in around 1140, when Wernibald was granted land in the area by his liege lord, Hugh de Morville, Constable of Scotland. Subsequently, the Cunninghams acquired many other estates, including Glencairn, which became an earldom in 1488. The Cunninghams supported the Stewarts and in 1653, the 8th Earl raised an army in the Highlands in support of the exiled King Charles II. Later, after Charles' restoration in 1660, the Earl became Lord Chancellor of Scotland.

MODERN CUNNINGHAM TARTAN

Dalziel/Dalzell

• The basic form of the Dalziel tartan was used for the 'George IV' tartan of 1822.

• The name Dalziel, frequently pronounced as 'D.L.', means 'I dare'.

The Dalziel clan name has undergone around 200 changes of spelling since 1259. It derives from the barony of Dalziel, which was held in 1288 by Hugh, Sheriff of Lanark. The family was ennobled in 1639, when Robert Dalziel was created 1st Earl of Carnwath after purchasing the Carnwath estates from the Earl of Mar in 1630. The senior branch of the clan was Dalziel of Binns, founded by Thomas Dalziel, a charismatic character who became a general in the Russian army and established the Regiment of Royal Scots Greys in 1678. The Dalziel estate in West Lothian was made into a barony in 1685.

MODERN DALZIEL TARTAN

Davidson

• There are two versions of the Davidson Clan tartan – the Half Davidson (top right) in which the pattern is reduced; and the Double Davidson, in which the red and white stripes are doubled.

• The 2nd Laird of Tulloch, Duncan Davidson, was a great favourite of Queen Victoria.

There were several Davidson lines in Scotland, including the Davidsons of Tulloch, who acquired the castle of Tulloch in the 18th century. The most prominent Davidson line was Davidson of Badenoch, or Clan Dhai as the family was also known. Davidson of Tulloch was the name of Robert the Bruce's rival for the Scots throne, John Comyn. Known as the Red Comyn, he was killed by Bruce in 1306. Whether as Comyn, Clan Dhai or Davidson, however, these people were trouble. After becoming attached to the Clan Chattan confederation, they were involved in several vicious feuds, notably with the MacPhersons. Eventually, Davidson power went into serious decline and the clan lost cohesion.

ANCIENT DAVIDSON TARTAN

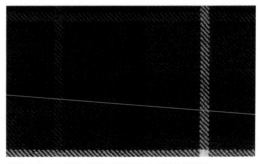

MODERN DAVIDSON OF TULLOCH TARTAN

Douglas

• The famous Scots novelist Sir Walter Scott used the castle of the Clan Douglas as the model for his *Castle Dangerous*, which was published in 1832.

• In Gaelic, the name Douglas, which derives from the dale south of Lanark, means 'black water'.

ANCIENT DOUGLAS TARTAN

The first Douglas to be recorded, between 1175 and 1199, was William de Duglas. The Douglases became one of Scotland's most powerful families, noted for their role in the struggle for Scots independence. Sir James Douglas, also known as 'Black Douglas', died while attempting to take Robert the Bruce's heart to the Holy Land in 1330. The Black Douglases remained dominant until 1452, when William, the 8th Earl of Douglas defied King James II and was killed by the monarch himself. After that Douglas power shifted to a rival branch, the Red Douglases, who were led by George Douglas, 4th Earl of Angus.

MODERN DOUGLAS GREY TARTAN

Drummond

• Drummonds could wear the tartans of other clans – for example, the Ogilvie tartan, which was worn by the Drummonds of Strathallen.

• The Drummonds were one of several families living on the edge of the Highlands of Scotland.

The parish of Drymen ('high ground' in Gaelic) is reputed to be the origin of the name Drummond. The first Drummond chief, Malcolm Beg, was Chamberlain of Lennox. Although Drummonds swore fealty to King Edward I in 1296, the family later supported Robert the Bruce and were rewarded with lands in Perthshire. The Drummonds acquired royal connections in 1357. This laid the foundations for later Drummond power, which included a peerage for Sir John, created Lord Drummond in 1488. James, the 4th Lord Drummond, was made Earl of Perth in 1605. The earldom became a dukedom in 1693. The family supported the Stewart monarchy and the second and the third Dukes of Perth fought for the Jacobite cause in 1715 and 1745.

MODERN DRUMMOND TARTAN

MODERN DRUMMOND OF PERTH TARTAN

Dunbar

• The Dunbar tartan was first recorded in *Vestiarium Scoticum* in 1842.

• The Clan Dunbar, whose name means 'the fort on the point', originated near the Scots-English border.

The progenitor of the clan, whose earldom of Dunbar dated from the 11th century, was Crinan the Thane, father of King Duncan I, who was murdered by Macbeth in 1040. Other involvements with Scotland's kings were no less dramatic. Patrick 'Blackbeard', 2nd Earl of Dunbar, failed to win the Scots crown, losing to Robert the Bruce: Blackbeard's wife belonged to the rival Comyn family. Eventually, royalty ruined the Dunbars. King James I coveted the Dunbar estates and to get them, falsey accused George Dunbar, the 11th Earl, of treason. The estates were never recovered.

MODERN DUNBAR TARTAN

Duncan

• **The Clan Duncan tartan has an additional name, Leslie of Wardis.**

• **Admiral Adam Duncan was created a viscount by King George III in 1800.**

The Duncan family were descended from the ancient Earls of Atholl. Originally known as Clann Connachaidh, they took their name from Donnachaidh Reamhar, or 'Fat Duncan', who led them at the Battle of Bannockburn in 1314. The Duncans were both powerful and prominent, with lands in Forfarshire and Angus, which included the Gourdie estate and the barony of Lundie. They gained great prestige in the 18th century for their service in the Hanoverian navy: Adam Duncan took part in the defeat of the Spaniards at Cape St. Vincent in 1780 and followed this with the defeat of the Dutch fleet at Camperdown in 1797.

MODERN DUNCAN TARTAN

Dundas

• The Dundas tartan, first known date 1842, is a traditional Highland military tartan.

• The Dundas clan played an important part in restoring the traditional Highland way of life after the penalties incurred as a result of the 1745 rebellion.

The Dundas family is an old one and can be traced to a son of Gospatrick, an 11th-century Prince of Northumberland. Shortly afterwards, the Dundas family settled north of the border, in Scotland. By 1296, they were eminent enough for Serle and Robertus de Dundas to be required to swear fealty to King Edward I. Sir James Dundas was made governor of Berwick in the late 15th century. Later clansmen include Robert Dundas of Arniston, appointed a judge in 1689, and two Lords President of the Court of Sessions.

MODERN DUNDAS TARTAN

Elliot

• The blue and maroon colours of the Elliot tartan, first recorded in 1906, make it unique among traditional Scots tartans.

• The Elliots, a Border clan, moved to Teviotdale from Glenshie in the early 14th century.

In the 15th century, there was a record of one Elliot of Redheugh, possibly an ancestor of Robert Elliot of Redheugh, described as the 10th chief of the clan. Unfortunately, much of the later history of the Elliott's is concerned with their violent feud with the neighbouring Scott clan. This feud began in 1565, when four members of the Elliot clan were executed by the Scotts of Buccleuch for rustling cattle. The Elliot's revenge was savage and might well have continued to escalate had the Scotts not thought better of the quarrel and opted to settle it by more diplomatic means.

MODERN ELLIOT TARTAN

Erskine

• The Erskine clan tartan, which dates from 1842, resembles the Cunningham and MacGregor tartans.

• There are other Erskine tartans, including a black-and-white dress tartan (bottom right).

The Renfrewshire barony of Erskine, source of the family name, was a title held by Henry de Erskyn during the reign of Alexander II in the first half of the 13th century. The clan was close to the Scots royal family for many generations, especially after Thomas, a brother of Robert the Bruce, married the eldest daughter of Sir John de Irskyn. Henceforth, the Bruce family could always count on unswerving support from the Clan Erskine. In the 15th century, Sir Robert Erskine was created Lord Erskine. The 6th Lord Erskine, who had once been her tutor, was created Earl of Mar by Mary, Queen of Scots. Sadly, the earldom was a casualty of the Jacobite rebellion of 1715, when John Erskine, 6th Earl of Mar, supported James Edward Stewart, the 'Old Pretender', resulting in the forfeiture of his title.

MODERN ERSKINE TARTAN

MODERN ERSKINE BLACK-AND-WHITE TARTAN

Farquharson

• The Farquharson tartan, for which the earliest known date is 1774, was based directly on the Black Watch tartan.

• The Farquharson clan, part of the confederation of Clan Chattan, was of Celtic origin.

Farquhar, son of Shaw of Rothiemurchus, gave his name to this clan, which settled in the area around Strathdee in Aberdeenshire. Although his children adopted the name Farquharson, many clan members continued to use the surname Shaw. Farquharsons supported the Stewart monarchy and fought under the banner of James Graham, Marquis of Montrose. Farquharson battle honours included Worcester in 1651, where the future King Charles II was defeated and forced to flee into exile. The Farquharsons of Invercauld supported both the Jacobite rebellions, in 1715 and 1745, and fought at Culloden in 1746.

ANCIENT FARQUHARSON TARTAN

Ferguson

• The Ferguson tartan may have been based on the old Lochaber district tartan.

• Anne Laurie, heroine of the famous song, was the wife of Ferguson of Craigdarroch.

The Ferguson clan, which was Celtic in origin, was established in Perthshire, Aberdeenshire, Fife, Ayrshire, Dumfriesshire and Argyllshire. The Fergusons of Perthshire were recognized as the principle Highland branch. Another branch, the Fergusons of Craigdarroch, can trace their ancestry back to Fergus, a 12th-century Prince of Galloway, and have held their ancestral lands since the 15th century. A Ferguson maverick, Robert the Plotter, was one of the Rye House conspirators, who, in 1683, planned to kill King Charles II and his brother, the future James VII (of Scotland) and II (of England and Ireland).

ANCIENT FERGUSON TARTAN

Fletcher

• This pattern (top right) is a general tartan for everyone surnamed Fletcher.

• The tartan is similar to the Old Lochaber district clan: Lochaber includes Glenorchy, where the Fletchers were the first Scots clan to settle.

Clan Fletcher were named for their skills as fletchers, or arrow-makers. In Argyll, Fletchers were associated with the Stewarts and the Campbells. The Fletchers proved useful in other ways. In 1497, they recovered cattle belonging to the Stewarts, which had been rustled by the MacDonalds. This earned the clan the gratitude of Stewart of Appin, who pledged to help the Fletchers. Around 1600, the bond of friendship was formalized when the Fletchers and Campbells in Glenorchy, where both clans lived, entered into a bond. The Fletchers were never a substantial clan, but their profession scattered them, and saw to it that branches of the clan proliferated. Fletchers from Achallader, at the head of Glenorchy, settled in Dunans, where they became an important family in the 18th and 19th centuries.

MODERN FLETCHER TARTAN

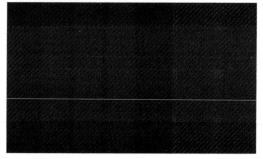

MODERN FLETCHER-DUNANS TARTAN

Forbes

• Tradition says the Forbes tartan was designed by a Miss Forbes in 1822, but the pattern appears in Wilson's pattern book earlier, in 1819.

• The name Forbes comes from the Gaelic word for 'field' – *forba*.

This clan takes its name and derives from the Forbes lands in Aberdeenshire. It is thought to be descended from Ochonobar, a Celt who won the future Forbes lands by saving the local villagers from a giant bear that had been terrorizing them. Sadly, this colourful story is not supported by historical evidence: the lands, it seems, were not in Forbes ownership as early as Celtic times, but were acquired only in the 13th century. The clan had a record for resisting intrusions across the border with England. In 1303, Alexander of Forbes died when the army of the English King Edward I attacked Urquhart Castle. In 1332, his son was killed at the battle of Dupplin Muir. Most Forbes clansmen supported the efforts of the exiled Stuart dynasty to regain their throne.

MODERN FORBES DRESS TARTAN

ANCIENT FORBES TARTAN

Forsyth

• The Forsyth tartan is similar to the Leslie, except that it has yellow instead of white.

• The seal adopted by David Forsyth of Dykes after 1488 closely resembled the arms of the Norman Viscomte de Fronsac.

The Clan Forsyth's origins may be Celtic or Norman – from the Gaelic *fearsith*, meaing 'man of peace', or from Forsach, the name of a Viking settler in northern France. In 1236, Viscomte de Fronsoc accompanied Eleanor of Provence to England to marry King Henry III. Later, the de Fronsocs acquired lands in Northumberland, Stirlingshire and Lanarkshire. Branches of the Forsyth clan then became established throughout Ayrshire and around Glasgow, and in the 16th century, gained royal connections when James Forsyth married a great-grand daughter of King James III.

MODERN FORSYTH TARTAN

Fraser

• This may be an early Clan Grant tartan, seen in an 18th-century portrait of Robert Grant of Lurg.

• The tartan with the brown background (bottom right) is the Fraser hunting tartan.

The Clan Fraser is reputed to trace its descent back to either the Angevins of Anjou in northern France or to the Normans, although the name Fraser was not known in Scotland until the 12th century. In the Highlands, Sir Andrew Fraser acquired the lands of Lovat through his marriage to the daughter of the Earl of Orkney and Caithness. The Fraser clan became established in the Highlands and in 1431, Sir Hugh Fraser of Lovat, Sheriff of Inverness, was created Lord Fraser of Lovat. The son of Lord Lovat commanded forces in the Jacobite rebellion of 1745 at Culloden. The father was executed and though the son was pardoned, the Fraser title was attainted.

FRASER TARTAN

ANCIENT FRASER HUNTING TARTAN

Galbraith

• This Galbraith tartan has also been named as Russell, Hunter and Mitchell. It dates from 1816.

• In Gaelic, the surname 'Galbraith' may have meant a 'strange' or 'foreign Briton' or simply the 'son of a Briton'.

Initial mention of the Galbraiths in Scotland was in 1208, when one Gillescop Galbraith witnessed a charter for Malduin, the Lord of Lennox. Malduin and Galbraith may have been related, since a 12th- century charter of Alwin, Earl of Lennox, mentioned one Gillespie Galbraith as *nepote nostro*, or 'our nephew'. The ancestor of the Galbraiths may therefore have been a Briton from the north, who crossed the Scots border to settle in Strathclyde. The principal Galbraith family was established at Baldernock, and the Galbraiths of Culcreuch, the builders of a famous castle, were their descendants.

ANCIENT GALBRAITH TARTAN

63

Gordon

• **This is a regimental tartan dating from 1793.**

• **Other Gordon tartans include the Red Gordon, the Old Huntly and the Gordon of Abergeldie.**

The name Gordon comes from *gor-dun*, which means 'hill fort' and derives from Berwickshire. However, in the 14th century the Gordons moved north into Aberdeenshire where the Lord of Gordon, Sir Adam Gordon, became a friend of Scots hero William Wallace. Sir Adam was granted lands in Huntly or Strathbogie by Robert the Bruce as reward for the clan's efforts in the war of independence against the English. The direct male line of the Gordon clan came to an end with a later Adam Gordon, whose only child was a girl, Elizabeth. However, she married one Alexander Seton and he later assumed the surname Gordon. The son of Adam and Elizabeth Gordon was created Earl of Huntly in 1449. This line died out with the 5th Duke, but the earldom of Aberdeen, a title conferred in 1682 continued, and later produced a Governor General of Canada.

MODERN GORDON TARTAN

ANCIENT GORDON TARTAN

Gow

• The design on which this tartan was based features in portraits of Neil Gow by Sir Henry Raeburn.

• Neil Gow, who lived from 1727 to 1807, was known as 'the prince of Scottish fiddlers'.

Gobha, a Gaelic word meaning blacksmith or armourer, is the origin of the clan name Gow, which also appears as MacGowan, meaning 'son of a smith'. Gow or MacGow feature among the surnames in several different clans. However, the senior branch is believed to be connected with the MacPhersons and the Clan Chattan. There was, however, a territorial difference between the Gows and the MacGowans. The Gows lived mainly in Perthshire and Inverness-shire, while the MacGowans, who were initially to be found in Stirling, Glasgow, Fife, Dumfries and the lowlands and in the 12th century at Nithsdale, were eventually scattered more widely. Neil Gow was not only a famous fiddler, but also the composer of immensely popular reels and dances. The same is true of his son, Nathaniel.

ANCIENT GOW TARTAN

MODERN GOW TARTAN

Graham

• Sir William de Graham was given lands in Abercorn and Dalkeith by the Scots King David I.

• The Graham of Menteith tartan first appeared in 1816.

MODERN GRAHAM-MENTEITH TARTAN

ANCIENT GRAHAM-MONTROSE TARTAN

MODERN GRAHAM-MONTROSE TARTAN

Tradition has it that the original Graham was a Caledonian warrior named Gramus, who breached the Antonine wall that the Roman invaders of Britain built to keep the Caledonians at bay. A more likely origin of the Grahams has been found in Normandy and the manor of Graegham (grey home), which featured in the Norman Domesday Book of 1086. The Grahams settled in Menteith and Montrose. William de Graham, progenitor of the Menteith branch, acquired the lands of Dalkeith in 1128. William's descendants gained further land in Landaff and in the 14th century Malise Graham was given the earldom of Menteith. The Montrose connection came about after the 14th century, when the Grahams acquired land in Kincardine and Old Montrose. William Graham became Earl of Montrose in 1504.

Grant

• The Grant clan tartan shown, dating from 1831, is sometimes called Drummond.

• It is difficult to establish a single Grant tartan: in 10 portraits of Grant brothers at Cullen House, Cullen, each wears a different tartan.

The Clan Grant is of Celtic origin and claims descent from the legendary 9th-century king, Kenneth MacAlpine. Grant influence in northeast Scotland became considerable and in the late 13th century the clan gave strong support to William Wallace. Later, they championed King Charles I, but in the Jacobite rebellions the clan's alliegance was divided. Most supported the Hanoverians, but the Grants of Glenmoriston were loyal to the Stewarts, and fought for Bonnie Prince Charlie at Culloden in 1746. Subsequently, many Glenmoriston Grants were banished to Barbados, in the West Indies.

MODERN GRANT TARTAN

Gunn

• **The MacKays were near neighbours of the Gunns and their tartans resemble each other.**

• **The Clan Gunn may have been the descendants of a Viking pirate.**

The Clan Gunn, whose ancestral territory lay in Caithness and Sunderland, claim to be Viking in origin. They may be descendants of the Norse King of Man and the Isles, Olave the Black, who died in 1237. An alternative progenitor of the Gunns was a Viking pirate who settled at Ulbster in Caithness. The name Gunn seems apt: it means 'battle', which the clan never avoided. They were involved in many feuds, notably with the Clan Keith. In 1426, the daughter of Lachlan Gunn was abducted to Ackergill by Clan Keith, where she threw herself from a tower. The Gunns and the Keiths then fought a hard but indecisive battle at Thurso. The feud burned on for almost another century until Gunn's grandson killed Keith of Ackergill, his son and 12 of his men at Drummoy in Sutherland.

MODERN GUNN TARTAN

ANCIENT GUNN TARTAN

Guthrie

• The Guthries were said to descend from a Viking named Guthrum, but their surname may have come from a Scots place name.

• The Guthries' feud with the Gardynes went on for 40 years.

The Guthrie clan, which settled in Gutherin, southeast Angus, probably adapted the place name as its own. Originally royal falconers, the Guthries later served in more prestigious capacities. In 1461, for instance, Sir David Guthrie was appointed Lord Treasurer of Scotland. The Guthries conducted a long feud with the neighbouring Clan Gardyne after Patrick Gardyne was killed by William Guthrie in 1578. The Gardynes answered by assassinating Alexander Guthrie in 1587. Over 30 years later, in 1618, after many more lives were lost on both sides, the Guthries were granted a royal pardon.

ANCIENT GUTHRIE TARTAN

Hamilton

• There may have been no Hamilton tartan before the design (top right) was recorded in 1842.

• In the Hamilton hunting tartan (bottom right) the red of the family sett was altered to green.

The Hamilton clan was founded by Walter, Fitz (son of) Gilbert de Hameldone, who was recorded on the Homage Roll of Renfrewshire in 1296. He later received the Barony of Cadzow in Lanarkshire from Robert the Bruce. In 1445, Sir James Hamilton, Lord of Cadzow was created Lord Hamilton by the Scots King James II. The Hamiltons acquired the earldom of Arran, in 1503 and in 1603 the Earldom of Abercorn was added. The clan's connection with the Stewart kings of Scotland was forged in 1474, when Sir James Hamilton married a daughter of James II. In 1651, William, 2nd Duke of Hamilton, supported the future King Charles I, but was killed at Worcester. His niece Anne succeeded him and she later married Lord William Douglas, whose family then inherited the Hamilton titles.

ANCIENT HAMILTON DRESS TARTAN

HAMILTON GREEN TARTAN

Hannay

• The earliest known date for the Hannay family tartan is around 1844, when Anne Hannay found an old kilt in a family chest.

• The Hannay clan originates from the ancient Celtic principality of Galloway.

The first Hannay to be recorded in Scotland was one Gilbert de Hannethe, who acquired the lands of Sorbie before 1296. Ultimately, Hannay power and influence became considerable and they dominated their lands by building a famous tower in around 1550. It became the seat of the Hannay clan chief, but became derelict after the Hannays were outlawed and the clan lands were lost in around 1640. This was the consequence of a protracted feud between the Hannays and the Murrays of Broughton, which ruined the clan and led to their large-scale emigration to Ulster.

HANNAY TARTAN

Hay and Leith

• **The modern version of the ancient Hay clan tartan was known as the Hay and Leith tartan. The Leiths were a sept of Clan Hay.**

• **The Hay and Leith tartan was first known some time between 1810 and 1820.**

The origins of the Clan Hay lie in the Cotentin Peninsula in northern France, where the powerful family once lived in the town of Le Haye. William de la Haye arrived in Scotland around 1160; he married a Celtic heiress and held the post of royal cup bearer. In about 1172, he was awarded the lands of Erroll by King William the Lion. The royal connections continued in later generations. Haye's grandson was Gilbert, 3rd Baron Erroll, who became Co-Regent of Scotland and was one of the heroes of the Scots struggle for independence. Robert the Bruce rewarded him with an appointment as hereditary Constable of Scotland. The seventh clan chief married a daughter of King Robert II and the Erroll title was elevated to an earldom in 1452.

MODERN HAY AND LEITH TARTAN

ANCIENT HAY TARTAN

Henderson

• The Clan Henderson lived in Lochaber and Angus, while those from northern Scotland were associated with the Clan Gunn.

• The Henderson tartan is similar to the Davidson tartan except that it has alternating white and yellow overchecks instead of red.

The Gaelic name McEanruig is sometimes 'translated' into English as MacKendrick, but its most familiar rendering is the surname Henderson, which means 'Henry's son'. The name apparently originated with a semi-mythical Pictish leader named Eanruig Mor mac Righ Neachtan, or 'Great Henry, son of King Nechtan'. Eanruig was supposedly the founder of the Glencoe branch of the Henderson clan, while George Gunn, who was killed in 1464 in a feud with the Keith family, has been named as the forefather of the Hendersons of Caithness. The Hendersons living in Glencoe were the more numerous of the two branches and lived in Glencoe long before the arrival of the clans MacLean and MacDonald.

ANCIENT HENDERSON TARTAN

ANCIENT HENDERSON TARTAN

Home

• The ancestors of Clan Home, one of the most formidable and prestigious of border clans, were the Anglo-Saxon princes of Northumberland.

• One member of Clan Home became Great Chamberlain of Scotland in 1488.

In 1605, the Homes were given an earldom by King James VI (of Scotland) and I (of England and Ireland). Much of their early clan history was violent. In 1516, Lord Home was accused of treason and lost his title. Both he and his brother were executed. Another brother, George Home, recovered the family estates, but he was killed before the battle of Pinkie in 1547 and the Home property was seized by the English. The 5th Lord Home, Alexander, recovered it two years later, but was then charged with treason against King James IV: he was released, however, died days later.

MODERN HOME TARTAN

Hunter

• The tartan shown, top right, is believed to have been worn by the Hunters of Peebleshire.

• In 1985, the Cochrane-Patrick family became chiefs of Clan Hunter and changed their name to Hunter of Hunterston.

Originally official huntsmen to the Dukes of Normandy, the ancestors of Clan Hunter came to England after the Norman conquest and travelled north in the 12th century with the Scots King David I. The Hunters were granted the lands of Hunter's Toune, modern Hunterston, in Ayrshire. In the 15th century, the Hunters were hereditary keepers of the royal forests in Arran and Cumbrae and Hunters to the King. The Hunter's long and faithful service was rewarded in 1375, when King Robert II gave William Hunter a charter for the barony and lands of AmeIe.

ANCIENT HUNTER TARTAN

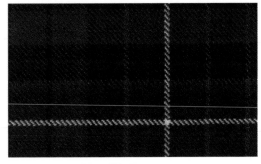

MODERN HUNTER TARTAN

Inglis

• The Inglis tartan is a variation of the MacIntyre tartan.

• The original MacIntyre pattern came from a doublet of 1800.

Inglis means 'English' – that is, 'southerners' who fled to Scotland to escape the Norman invaders after 1066. The family soon became prominent in Scotland. By 1296, Walter, John and Philip de Inglis were great magnates, owning considerable tracts of land. A century later, the family of Sir William Inglis, a champion performer at the tournament, received the barony of Manner by royal charter. Manner remained in the Inglis family until sold in 1708, by which time other members of the clan had grown rich enough to purchase the lands of Cramond from the Bishop of Dunkeld in 1624. Later, in 1680, John Inglis built a splendid mansion, Cramond House.

ANCIENT INGLIS TARTAN

Innes

• This red tartan is called the Innes tartan, while a similar hunting tartan with a mainly green background is called the MacInnes.

• The name Innes, adopted by the family in 1226, means 'greens'.

In 1160, a Flemish nobleman named Berowald was granted the barony of Innes in Morayshire after an agreement between King Malcolm IV and Somerled, Lord of the Isles. The family was officially recognized as a clan in 1579, but it had earned prestige some time before then. William Innes, the 15th Chief was a member of the Reformation Parliament in 1560. The Innes clan were strong supporters of the royal Stewarts, and one branch of the family, which acquired the baronetcy of Coxton in 1686, fought for the deposed dynasty in both Jacobite rebellions.

MODERN INNES TARTAN

Irvine

• This Irvine tartan shown may have been dated as early as 1889.

• In 1649, Alexander, the 10th Irvine Laird of Drum, almost became Earl of Aberdeen, but King Charles I was executed before he could confirm the appointment.

The name Irvine comes from the Old English personal name Erewine or Erwinne, first recorded in Scotland in the 12th century. By the time the family acquired their lands in Dumfriesshire, their name had changed to Irvine. Later on, the Irvines of Bonshaw were neighbours of the Bruce family of Lochmaben and provided strong support for Robert the Bruce and his claim to the Scots crown. As reward, William de Irvine was granted the royal forest of Drum in Aberdeenshire. Drum Castle, built by the Irvines, became the family seat.

ANCIENT IRVINE TARTAN

Johnston

• The Johnston tartan probably came from the Aberdeenshire Johnstones rather than those on the Lowland Borders, where tartans were generally unnamed.

• The Johnstons and the Maxwells fought a long, deadly feud.

The ancestral lands of Clan Johnston lay in the barony of Johnstoun in Annandale, where they belonged to Sir Gilbert de Johnstoun in the early 13th century. The clan received many honours for their support of the Stewarts. In 1633, Sir James Johnston of Johnstone was created Lord Johnston of Lochwood by King Charles I; in 1643, he acquired the further title of Earl of Hartfell. The 2nd Earl of Hartfell was given the revived earldom of Annandale by King Charles II, and his son was created Marquess of Annandale by King William III in 1701.

ANCIENT JOHNSTON TARTAN

MODERN JOHNSTON TARTAN

Keith

• The Clan Keith tartan is called the 'Keith and Austin'. Austin was a Clan Keith sept.

• The tartan began as a small check Wilson of Bannockburn pattern of 1815 named 'Austin'.

The ancestry of Clan Keith may have been Celtic or Norman. The Norman ancestry derived from Hervey, an adventurer who was granted the lands of Keith in Lothian in about 1150. After this the Keith family became prominent. In 1176, Hervey's son became Great Marischal of Scotland, a position that made him responsible for the safety of the Scots monarch and the royal regalia. The title remained in the Keith family for the next 700 years. In the 14th century, the Keiths acquired lands in Caithness by marriage, but a damaging feud with the Clan Gunn over land ownership followed. Nonetheless, the Keiths created a fine military tradition. In 1314, Sir Robert Keith led the cavalry charge that routed the English archers at Bannockburn. Keiths fought at Flodden in 1513 and in the Jacobite rebellion of 1715.

MODERN KEITH TARTAN

ANCIENT KEITH TARTAN

Kennedy

• **The Kennedy tartan, first recorded in 1845, was originally worn by the Kennedys of Lochaber.**

• **The tartan was later adopted by the Kennedys of Carrick as a sign of their Jacobite sympathies.**

In old Irish Gaelic, *cinneidigh*, the origin of the name Kennedy, is not particularly complimentary: it means 'ugly-headed'. The clan settled in the ancient Kingdom of Dalriada, however, many Kennedys later moved to Carrick in Ayrshire. Clan Kennedy descent, it is claimed, derives from the Earls of Carrick. The clan also asserts its kinship with the Bruce family, a claim arising from the marriage, in 1405, between James Kennedy and Mary, daughter of King Robert III. In 1509, the Kennedys acquired an earldom of their own when Sir David Kennedy was created Earl of Cassillis. Kennedy power achieved its apogee after the battle of Flodden in 1513. The first few Kennedy earls were, however, singularly unfortunate. The first died at Flodden. The second was murdered in 1527. The third, Gilbert Kennedy, was poisoned in 1558.

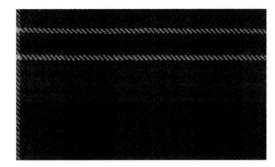

MODERN KENNEDY TARTAN

ANCIENT KENNEDY TARTAN

81

Kerr

• The Kerr tartan was first recorded in *Vestiarium Scoticum* in 1842, but may be much older.

• Kerr is Scandinavian. from the old Norse *Kjirri*, meaning 'marsh dweller'.

The Kerrs came to England with the Normans, who were themselves originally Scandinavian. Family tradition has it that the Kerrs arrived in Scotland when two brothers, Ralph and Robert, moved north from Lancashire into Roxburghshire. Ralph is said to be the ancestor of the Kerrs of Ferniehurst, and Ralph, the ancestor of the Kerrs of Cessford. Clan Kerr became royal vassals and in 1451, Andrew Kerr of Cessford acquired the barony of Old Roxburgh, which became a dukedom after 1707. The baronies of Oxnam and Newbattle, the Lordship of Lothian and the Earldom of Ancram also came within the scope of Clan Kerr.

MODERN KERR TARTAN

Kilgour

• The name Kilgour has several spellings, including Kilgo and Kilgore.

• Tradition has it that the origins of the Clan Kilgour lie in the Clan Douglas.

The Clan Kilgour takes its name from the ancient parish of Kilgour near Falkland in Fifeshire, where the earliest recorded Kilgour, Sir Thomas Kilgour, was chaplain of St. Thomas' Church. At first, the Kilgours were followers of the McDuff Earls of Fife, but they may have had an even closer connection with Clan Douglas. Legend suggests that an infant abandoned on the steps of St. Thomas Church was presumed to be a Douglas, placed there after the Douglas clan, already outlawed, had been almost wiped out in battle. The child later assumed the name Kilgour and, it appears, went on to propagate the Clan Kilgour.

ANCIENT KILGOUR TARTAN

MODERN KILGOUR TARTAN

Kincaid

• Traditionally, the Kincaids' ancestry relates them to several other Scots clans and families.

• Kincaid ancestry is said to link the clan to the Earls of Lennox, the Galbraiths, the Grahams and the Comyn Lords of Badenoch.

An early reference to Kincaid occurred in 1238, with a grant of the lands of Kincade to Maldouen, the third Earl of Lennox by King Alexander III. By 1280, the Kincaid territory stretched from the Glazert to the Kelvin rivers, an area thought to cover around 30,000 acres (120 square kilometres). Despite their traditional relationship with the Comyns, Robert the Bruce's rivals for the Scots crown, the Kincaids supported the Bruce's claim and one Kincaid so distinguished himself during the successful recapture of Edinburgh Castle from the English that he was made constable of the castle.

KINCAID TARTAN

Lamont

• The Lamont tartan is virtually the same as the Clan Forbes tartan, both of which originated with the design of the Black Watch.

• The name Lamont probably comes from the Norse *logmoor* (*lodhman* in Gaelic) meaning 'law-giver'.

The Clan Lamont may well be Viking in origin. The forbears of the Clan Lamont were reputedly the O'Neill princes of Tyrone in Ireland, a reflection of the great seafaring skills of Danish Vikings, who settled across Scotland and Ireland. The original Scots Lamont lands were in Argyll, but these were later poached by the Campbells and other clans. Eventually, the family was confined to Cowal, where one John Lamont became Bailie in 1456. The clan's territory was enlarged in 1539, when Sir John Lamont of Inveryne acquired the Barony of Inveryne. He took up residence at Toward Castle, but during the 17th-century civil war, the Campbells destroyed the castles at Ascog and Toward, and in 1646 they killed some 200 members of the clan at Dunoon.

ANCIENT LAMONT TARTAN

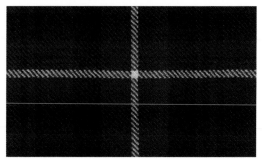

MODERN LAMONT TARTAN

Lauder

• The Lauder tartan first appeared in a collection of tartans dated around 1830.

• The Clan Lauder was Norman in origin.

Even before the conquest of 1066, there were numerous Normans at the court of the English King Edward the Confessor. It was here that the future Malcolm III hired a Norman knight, Sir Robert de Lavendre, to help unseat the usurper Macbeth, who had murdered his father, King Duncan. Mission was accomplished in 1057, and afterwards de Lavendre was rewarded with large grants of land in Berwickshire and Lothian.

His descendant William Lawedre was appointed Sheriff of Perth in the 13th century, when the family acquired Bass Rock in the Firth of Forth. The Lauders supported both William Wallace and Robert the Bruce in the struggle for Scots independence.

MODERN LAUDER TARTAN

Leslie

• The Clan Leslie tartan was first recorded in the Cockburn collection of 1810–1820.

• The name 'Lesslyn' (later Leslie) probably came from the Gaelic *leas cuilinn*, 'garden of holly'.

The Clan Leslie took its name from its ancestral lands, the Barony of Lesslyn. The progenitor of the clan was Bartolf, a Flemish noble. In the 12th century, he acquired the Barony of Lesly and was appointed governor of Edinburgh Castle by King Malcolm III. The surname Leslie was first taken by Norman, Bartolf's great-grandson. In the 15th century, another of Bartolf's descendants, George de Lesly of Rothes, was created the first Earl of Rothes. In the struggle between Catholics and the Presbyterian 'Covenanters' for control of the church in Scotland, General Alexander Leslie headed the Covenanter forces. In 1640 he invaded England, where he inflicted a heavy defeat on King Charles I's troops. However, King Charles was forced to mollify the Scots by creating Leslie Earl of Leven.

ANCIENT LESLIE TARTAN

MODERN LESLIE TARTAN

Lindsay

• Red backgrounds are common in tartans, but the crimson background in the Lindsay tartan is unusual.

• The Lindsay surname was first mentioned as early as the 11th century as 'Lindsay of Ercildon'.

The Lindsays, originally a Norman family, took their name from their Borders estate of Lindeseye. Sir William de Lindseye was a member of the retinue of King David I. His grandson, also named William, married the daughter of the Scots Prince Henry. This second William also acquired Crawford property in Lanarkshire, and in around 1340, his descendant, Sir David Lindsay, Laird of Crawford, married an heiress of the Earl of Angus, which meant that the Lindsays acquired the Angus estates, where the family moved from Clydesdale at the end of the 14th century. The elder son of Sir David, Alexander Lindsay of Glenesk, became first Earl of Crawford. In 1398, another Sir David Lindsay, of Glenesk, married into the Scots royal family, thus adding the Barony of Strathnairn in Inverness-shire.

ANCIENT LINDSAY TARTAN

WEATHERED LINDSAY TARTAN

Livingstone

• **The Livingstone tartan was probably copied from a relic of the 1745 Jacobite rebellion named MacDonnell of Keppoch.**

• **The 19th-century explorer David Livingstone was descended from the Livingstones of Appin, a small sept of the Stewarts of Appin.**

The lands of Levingstoun in West Lothian gave rise to the name Livingston. One example of a Livingston signature is found in the charter of the Earl of Lennox, dated 1270 and witnessed by Sir William Livingston of Gorgyn, near Edinburgh, the progenitor of the Livingston clan. In 1347, another Sir William Livingston married the heiress of Patrick de Callender, and acquired forfeit lands. In time, Sir William and Lady Livingston became the ancestors of the Livingstons of Westquarter and Kinnaird, Bonton and Dunipace. Another branch of the family acquired a noble title in 1600, when the 7th Lord Livingston was created Earl of Linlithgow. The earldom was lost after the Jacobite rebellion of 1715.

MODERN LIVINGSTON TARTAN

ANCIENT LIVINGSTON TARTAN

Logan

• **The Logan tartan illustrated right was first recorded in 1831.**

• **A much earlier tartan, which was at one time known as Logan, now has the name Skene.**

The Clan Logan has a dramatic and chequered history. In 1329, two of the Lowland Logans, Sir Robert and Sir Walter, were killed in a battle with the Moors in Spain while on a mission to take the heart of Robert the Bruce to the Holy Land. The principal base of the Lowland Logans in Scotland was at Restalrig, near Edinburgh. Sir Robert of Restalrig married a daughter of King Robert II and was appointed Admiral of Scotland in 1400. This greatly raised the status of the Logan clan, but ultimately the Lowland branch of Clan Logan was to meet with disaster. In 1582, the last Logan of Restalrig was outlawed and his lands confiscated for his part in the Gowrie conspiracy, in which King James VI was captured and held hostage by William Ruthven, Earl of Gowrie. Subsequently, Gowrie was executed.

ANCIENT LOGAN TARTAN

WEATHERED LOGAN TARTAN

Lumsden

• The Lumsden tartan shown is the most frequently worn 'short' version

• The lands of Lumisden in Berwickshire, first mentioned in the ancient records in 1098, came into the possession of Gillem and Cren de Lummisden around a century later.

The progenitor of the Clan Lumsden was Adam de Lumisden who, together with his son Roger, signed the Ragman Rolls, swearing alliegance to King Edward I in 1296. Adam was the first recognized chief of the Lumsden clan, and in time the family name spread to many areas of Scotland, including Airdrie, Innergellie, Stravithie, Lathallen, Rennyhill in Fifeshire and more territories in the north. One particularly important Lumsden possession was the territory of Blanerne, which was acquired in 1329 along with lands in Aberdeenshire.

MODERN LUMSDEN TARTAN

MacAlistair

• The earliest known date for the MacAlistair of Glenbarr tartan, which is the same as the MacGillivray hunting tartan, is 1930.

• The design of the MacAlistair of Glenbarr is related to the MacDonald group of tartans.

The clan's progenitor was Alastair Mor, great-grandson of Somerled, Lord of the Isles. His descendants settled in Kintyre, where Charles MacAlister became hereditary constable of the royal castle of Tarbert in 1481. Other branches were the MacAlisters of Loup, Menstrie and Glenbarr. In 1600, MacAlisters invaded the Isle of Arran, plundering the Montgomery estate of Skelmorie and making off with booty worth some £12,000. Royal Stewart property on the island was also ravaged. Afterwards, Alexander, leader of the MacAlisters, was hanged for treason in Edinburgh.

MODERN MACALISTAIR TARTAN

MacAlpine

• The earliest recorded source for the MacAlpine tartan is dated 1908.

• Except for its yellow lines, the MacAlpine tartan closely resembles the MacLean hunting tartan.

Although the MacAlpines are a small clan, they can boast the most distinguished of all forbears, Kenneth MacAlpine, who united the Scots and the Pictish crowns in the 9th century and so forged the beginnings of Scots state. Kenneth was the son of King Alpin of Dalriada, who was murdered after the Picts triumphed over the Scots in battle in 834 AD. As a result of Kenneth McAlpine's achievements, *Siol Alpine* – the race of Alpin – is a title claimed by many other clans, not all of them related to the MacAlpines. They include the MacGregors, Grants, MacKinnons, MacQuarries, MacNabs, MacDuffs or Macphies and the MacAulays.

ANCIENT MACALPINE TARTAN

MacArthur

• The MacArthur tartan reflects the clan's one-time link with the MacDonalds: it has the same basic form as the MacDonald of the Isles tartan.

• It is claimed that the MacArthurs represent an ancient branch of the Clan Campbell.

Traditionally, the MacArthurs, descended from ancient British or Celtic stock, are among the oldest of all clans in Argyllshire. The MacArthurs greatly increased their territory through their support for Robert the Bruce in the Scots wars of independence. Their chief was made hereditary Captain of the Castle of Dunstaffnage. However, the clan lost power after 1427, when chief John MacArthur was beheaded by King James I and his lands were made forfeit. Scots historian David Stewart of Garth suggested in the early 19th century that there was another clan MacArthur, whose chief lands were sited close to Loch Awe in Argyllshire. A further MacArthur family served as hereditary pipers to the MacDonalds of Sleat and were rewarded with lands on the island of Skye.

ANCIENT MACARTHUR TARTAN

MODERN MACARTHUR TARTAN

MacAulays

• The MacAulays of Ardincaple were associated with the MacGregors, and their tartan resembles that of the MacGregors.

• The MacAulays of Lewis (unrelated to the Ardincaples) were associated with the MacLeods.

Two branches of the MacAulay clan have very different origins. The MacAulays of Lewis claimed Olaf the Black, the Viking King of Man, as their ancestor. The other MacAulays were of Celtic origin and were at first known as Ardincaples in Dunbartonshire. The Ardincaples acquired a chief named Aulay and the clan took his name, as 'sons of Aulay' or MacAulay. Aulay was the brother of the Earl of Lennox and in 1296, Aulay was among the Scots nobles who signed the Ragman Rolls, confirming their duty of homage to King Edward I of England. The 'Celtic' MacAulays retained their lands at Ardincaple until 1767, when they were sold to the Duke of Argyll by the 12th chief of the clan. The MacAulays of Lewis fared less well, ending among the list of 'broken' Scots clans in 1594.

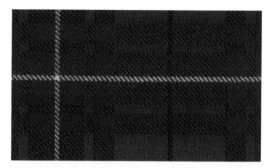

MODERN MACAULAY TARTAN

ANCIENT MACAULAY HUNTING TARTAN

MacBean, MacBain, MacVean

• The Clan MacBean tartan shown was described as 'Birrell Sett' by the artist R.R. MacIan.

• Around 1900, the McBean clan chief, who did not recognize the MacIan tartan as genuine, insisted on wearing the Mackintosh tartan instead.

The Clan MacBean claims descent from the 8th-century House of Moray. The MacBeans apparently originated in Lochaber but later settled in east Inverness-shire. They were associated with the Mackintoshes and supported that clan against John Comyn, Robert the Bruce's rival for the Scots crown. Many MacBeans fought and died on the Mackintosh side in the battle of Harlaw in 1411.

The MacBeans were exceptionally warlike. During the Jacobite Rebellion of 1745, one Giles MacBean killed 14 Hanoverian soldiers before being cut down himself.

MACBEAN TARTAN

MacBeth

• The MacBeth tartan is based on the Royal Stewart tartan and is sometimes called the Blue Stewart.

• The MacBeths were an ancient Celtic clan, taking their name from beatha, which was Gaelic for 'life'.

Macbeth, William Shakespeare's tragedy written in 1606, has ensured that the name of its eponymous anti-hero is among the most widely known of the Scots clans. The real MacBeth was a grandson of King Malcolm II and had a legitimate claim to the Scots throne. According to tradition, the MacBeths were affiliated to the Macdonalds, the MacLeans and the the MacBeans. However, there is considerable confusion about the clan's history, due mainly to the use of several names, including the anglicized Beaton and the adoption of McVeigh in place of MacBeth.

MODERN MACBETH TARTAN

MacCallum/ Malcolm

• The MacCallum tartan dates from at least 1822, almost as far back as tartans can be dated.

• Zachary MacCallum, a famous strong man, killed seven men in battle in 1647 before being attacked and killed from behind with a scythe.

The MacCallum name, like Malcolm, denotes the followers of St. Columba, who converted the Scots to Christianity in the 6th century. In time, McCallum and Malcolm became so closely linked that they were considered one clan. And then Dugald MacCallum of Poltralloch, who acquired the family lands in 1779, changed his surname to Malcolm. The MacCallums rose to prominence after Ronald MacCallum of Corbarron was granted lands in Craignish in 1414: these came with the hereditary post of constable at Lochaffy and Craignish Castle.

ANCIENT MACCALLUM TARTAN

MacColl

• The McColl tartan, then known as Old Bruce, was first known in 1797.

• The tartan is similar to that of the MacColls' allies, the Stewarts of Appin.

The Clan McColl, traditionally a branch of the mighty Clan MacDonald, inhabited the area around Loch Fyne from very early times. They also forged other clan connections, with the Stewarts of Appin and the MacGregors, among others. MacColl support for the MacGregors involved the clan in a fearful disaster in 1602, when the MacGregors' deadly rivals, the MacPhersons, ambushed them while they were returning home from a raid: the MacColls lost most of their men and the chief. They sustained further losses during the 1745 Jacobite rebellion, when they fought for the Stewarts of Appin and lost 18 killed and 15 wounded.

MODERN MACCOLL TARTAN

MacDiarmid

• The tartan of the Clan MacDiarmid, a sept of Clan Campbell, was first recorded in 1906.

• In Gaelic, MacDiarmid means 'son of Diarmid' or 'son of Dermot': Diarmid or Dermot means 'freedman'.

The popular Scots and Irish name Diarmid is held by numerous, not always related, families. The MacDiarmids of Glenlyon once claimed to be the most ancient bearers of the name. In the 18th century, several Glenlyon MacDiarmids joined the Duke of Atholl's Fencibles. To add to the confusion, the name can be spelled in different ways, including Mac Dermit, MacDerment, MacDiarmond or Mac Diarmond. There is even a record of one Nemeas MacTarmayt, the rector of Durnish in 1427, and in 1533, the curiously named Jhone McChormeit of Menyenis put his signature to a legal document.

MODERN MACDIARMID TARTAN

MacDonalds

• This MacDonald tartan (top right), dating from c.1815, was based on the Old Lochaber district sett.

• The Clanranald tartan (bottom right) dates from around 1816. The MacDonalds of Boisdale were a cadet branch of Clanranald.

The MacDonalds were the most powerful of the Highland clans. Named after Donald, the grandson of King Somerled of the Isles, the MacDonalds were prominent landowners, Lords of the Isles and, ultimately, Earls of Ross. During the struggle for Scots independence led by Robert the Bruce, the MacDonalds were divided, when Angus Og, brother of the clan chief Alexander, chose to fight on the Bruce's side at the battle of Bannockburn in 1314. The loyal Angus was rewarded with all Alexander's lands. The MacDonalds of Clanranald take their name from Ranald, younger son of John, 1st Lord of the Isles. Ranald acquired the North Isles among other lands in 1373 and afterwards founded the Moidart, Morar, Knoidart and Glengarry families.

MODERN MACDONALD TARTAN

ANCIENT MACDONALD TARTAN

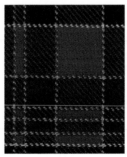

MODERN MACDONALD
OF BOISDALE TARTAN

ANCIENT MACDONALD
OF CLANRANALD TARTAN

MacDonald of the Isles/Sleat

• The clan tartan of MacDonald of the Isles is the MacDonald of Sleat sett with extra black overcheck.

• The MacDonald of Sleat, first known in around 1815, was called MacDonald of Sleat, Lord of the Isles tartan.

ANCIENT MACDONALD OF THE ISLES HUNTING TARTAN

The history of the MacDonalds of the Isles begins with the progenitor of all the MacDonalds, Somerled. Both the MacDonalds and the Mac Ruries descend from Reginald, Somerled's son. In 1430, Alexander, 3rd Lord of the Isles, inherited the earldom of Ross, and his son John, the 4th Lord, then tried to make the Isles independent. In 1493, the MacDonalds lost the lordship and the earldom, and the Isles line ended when the dispossessed 4th Lord died with no legitimate heirs. The progenitor of the MacDonalds of Sleat was Hugh, youngest son of Alexander, 3rd Lord of the Isles.

MODERN MACDONALD OF SLEAT TARTAN

MacDonnell of Glengarry

• The earliest date for the MacDonnell of Glengarry tartan is 1816.

• This tartan is the same as the basic Clan MacDonald sett, differing only by the addition of a white stripe.

'MacDonnell' is an alternative spelling of 'MacDonald' and appertains to two branches of the MacDonald clan: the MacDonnells of Glengarry and the MacDonnells of Keppoch. The Glengarry MacDonnells were founded by Alistair, grandson of Ranald, so giving the clan a common ancestor with the Clanranald MacDonalds. Alistair's descendants took formal possession of the Glengarry lands in 1539, and in 1627 the lands became a barony. the Stewart cause in the civil wars and Angus, 9th of Glengarry was rewarded in 1660 with the title Lord McDonnell and Aros.

ANCIENT MACDONNELL OF GLENGARRY TARTAN

103

MacDougall

• The Scottish Tartan Society archives contain 13 MacDougall setts.

• Like the MacDonalds, the MacDougalls were descended from Somerled, King of the Isles, through that monarch's eldest son, Dugall.

Alexander, grandson of Dugall, progenitor of the MacDougalls, married a daughter of John Comyn. This placed the MacDougalls on a collision course with Comyn's rival for the Scots crown, Robert the Bruce. Once the Bruce triumphed at Bannockburn in 1314 and secured the throne, he moved quickly to punish the MacDougalls. Alexander was forced to make submission to the new King, and after fleeing to England, his son John MacDougall of Lorn was captured in the Western Isles and imprisoned. John was released only after Robert's death in 1329, but later married his captor's grand-daughter.

MODERN MACDOUGALL TARTAN

MacDuff

• The MacDuff tartan is a version of the Royal Stewart tartan, simplified by the removal of the Stewart's white and yellow lines.

• The tartan is very similar to the tartan named for 'Bonnie Prince Charlie'.

Usually regarded as the oldest clan in Scotland, the MacDuffs trace their Celtic descent from the 10th-century King Dubh, or Duff. The family earldom of Fife was unusual in that it was held 'by the Grace of God'. A more likely first Earl was that same MacDuff who opposed Macbeth and featured in Shakespeare's tragedy. After Macbeth was killed in 1057, MacDuff helped King Malcolm III Canmore ascend the throne. The clan was rewarded with privileges including the right to crown Scots kings at their coronation and leadership of the Scots army. However, the MacDuffs became disaffected and, in 1306, Duncan, Earl of Fife declared his opposition to Robert the Bruce. In 1353, the earldom of Fife became extinct, although the title was later revived in 1735 in the peerage of Ireland.

MODERN MACDUFF TARTAN

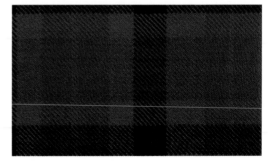

ANCIENT MACDUFF HUNTING TARTAN

MacEwan

• The MacEwan tartan, first recorded in 1906, resembles the Campbell tartan.

• The Clan MacEwan trace their ancestry from the Irish kings and the 5th-century Celtic Kingdom of Dalriada.

Before 1450, MacEwans were already chiefs of Otter, having acquired their name in the 13th century from Ewan of Otter. In 1432, however, the Campbells began to take over the MacEwan inheritance when they acquired the lands and barony of Otter. Subsequently, the MacEwans scattered. Some remained with the Campbells, joined the MacLachlans or became associated with the Colquhouns and the Camerons in Lochaber. However, some MacEwans acquired new territory, when they were given free lands in Lorne as reward for their role as hereditary bards to the Campbells.

ANCIENT MACEWAN TARTAN

MacFarlane

• The MacFarlane tartan dates from 1822, and is recorded at the Scottish Tartans Museum in Comrie, Perthshire.

• The Clan MacFarlane has Celtic roots, with ancestral territory sited on Loch Lomond.

The progenitor of the Clan MacFarlane was Alwyn, Earl of Lennox. It was Alwyn's great-grandson, Parlan, who gave the clan its name. The warlike MacFarlanes lost the earldom of Lennox after 1425, when Duncan, the last of the Celtic earls, and his sons were executed by King James I. The executions ended the male line of Lennox, but instead of awarding the vacant earldom to the MacFarlanes, who had a strong claim, James gave it to a relative, John Stewart, Lord Darnley. Pragmatically, Andrew MacFarlane, the 10th Chief, married Lord Darnley's daughter and reconnected the clan to the Lennox title. Nonetheless, the MacFarlanes met disaster in 1608, when after killing Colquhoun of Luss, the clan was outlawed and their name was forbidden.

WEATHERED MACFARLANE TARTAN

MODERN MACFARLANE TARTAN

MacFie

• The MacFie clan tartan, first recorded in 1906, was not finally registered by the Lord Lyon in Edinburgh until 1991.

• The MacFie name can also be spelled MacPhie, MacPhee or MacDuffie.

The Clan MacFie were once hereditary record keepers to the Lords of the Isles. They held lands on the Isle of Colonsay until the MacDonalds removed them in the mid-17th century. One branch of the clan became attached to Clan Cameron of Lochiel and fought with them at the battle of Culloden in 1746; unfortunately, they took severe losses while attempting to annihilate the left wing of the Hanoverian army. Later, the MacFies were widely scattered by the notorious Highland Clearances of 1763–1775, in which the English evicted families from the Highlands and the Isles of Scotland.

MODERN MACFIE TARTAN

MacGill

• A sample of the MacGill tartan kept in The Scottish Tartan Society's archives is dated sometime between 1930 and 1950.

• The name MacGill is thought to derive from Mac an ghoill, or 'son of a stranger'.

The Clan MacGill lived in Galloway and the Isle of Man from early times and afterwards settled in Jura. They achieved dubious prominence after 1566, when James MacGill of Rankeillor, Provost of Edinburgh, was implicated in the assassination of David Rizzio, secretary to Mary, Queen of Scots. As a devout Presbyterian, McGill hated the Catholic Queen Mary. After she abdicated and fled south to become a prisoner in England, it was James MacGill who gave Queen Elizabeth I the Casket Letters that implicated Mary in the murder of her second husband, Lord Darnley, in 1567.

ANCIENT MACGILL TARTAN

MODERN MACGILL TARTAN

MacGillivray

• The McGillivray tartan, known since 1816 and first recorded in 1831, has been described as 'typically Chattan'.

• The name MacGillivray means 'son of the servant of judgement'.

The Clan MacGillivray was an early branch of the Clan Chattan confederation. Their progenitor, Gillivray, a warrior whose fortress was at Dunmaglass in Strathnairn, could not resist the attempts of King Alexander II to impose royal authority in the Highlands. Around 1268, therefore, he put himself and his clan under the protection of Clan Chattan. The MacGillivrays settled at Dunmaglass around 1500, and a branch lived in Mull and Morven. The clan supported the Jacobite rebellions of 1715 and 1745, and at Culloden in 1746 nearly wiped out the left wing of the English army.

MODERN MACGILLIVRAY TARTAN

MacGregors

• The MacGregor tartan (top right) was listed in 1819 as the 'MacGregor Murray tartan'.

• The Rob Roy MacGregor tartan (bottom right) was first recorded in about 1815.

The first land held by the MacGregors, at Glenorchy, was once Campbell property, but had been given to the clan by a grateful King Alexander II after the conquest of Argyll. Over time their territory on the dangerous border of Argyll and Perthshire grew. The vengeful Clan Campbell joined with the Colquhouns and filched much MacGregor territory. Hostilities deepened until, in 1602 at Glenfruin, the MacGregors slaughtered 200 Colquhouns. The MacGregor name was abolished, although it was restored in 1775 by an Act of Parliament due to the efforts of Sir John MacGregor Murray. The simple red-and-black check tartan was supposedly worn by the renowned Scots hero Rob Roy MacGregor (1671–1734), who took part in the 1715 Jacobite rebellion, and was the subject of Sir Walter Scott's novel of 1817.

ANCIENT MACGREGOR TARTAN

ANCIENT MACGREGOR HUNTING TARTAN

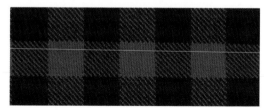

ANCIENT MACGREGOR – ROB ROY TARTAN

MacHardy

• Tradition has it that the Clan MacHardy of northeast Scotland were a race of giants.

• The MacHardys have been described as 'a wild and extravagant race'.

The McHardys clan members were the sort of men from which legends are made, but their legendary physical size had real-life foundation. It seems that the MacLeod chief on the island of Raasay hand-picked his biggest men to fight for the Earl of Mar. These men recognized the MacLeod as their chief, but acquired a name of their own after an encounter with Malcolm Canmore, who became King of Scotland in 1057. The MacLellans' bravery so impressed the King that he said: 'Hardy thou art and hardy thou shalt be!' The MacHardys, as they were from then on, were often chosen to lead raids into Badenoch.

MODERN MACHARDY TARTAN

MacIans

• Branches of the Clan MacIans are descended from the MacDonalds.

• This tartan first appeared in the *Vestiarium Scoticum* of 1842, and, though unlike other MacDonald tartans, is the most frequently produced MacDonald of Glencoe sett.

The Clan MacIan is connected to the MacDonalds. The 14th-century MacDonald chief, Eoin Sprangac, was the ancestor of the MacIans of Ardnamurchan, also known as the MacDonalds of Ardnamurchan. A further link was to the MacDonalds of Glencoe: the MacIans of Glencoe took their name from Iain Abrach, son of Angus Og. The connection was fatal: Alasdair MacDonald, the 12th Chief of the MacIan clan, died at Glencoe, where the MacDonalds were massacred by their hereditary enemies, the Campbells (with the connivance of the English).

MODERN MACIAN TARTAN

MacInnes

• This tartan with a green background belongs to the Clan MacInnes: the tartan with the red background is known under the name of Innes.

• Although MacInnes of the West and Innes of Moray are two separate clans, both wear the same setts as dress and hunting tartans.

The Clan MacInnes is of ancient Celtic origin, and once belonged to the *Siol Gillebride*, the earliest inhabitants of Morven and Ardnamurchan in Argyll. In the 12th century, the MacInnes and MacGillivray clans fought under King Somerled of the Isles against the Viking invaders. Many of the MacInnes chiefs served as constables of Kinlochaline Castle and one was in charge in 1645 during the civil wars, when the castle was besieged and burned. One branch of the clan were hereditary bowmen to the MacKinnons.

MODERN MACINNES HUNTING TARTAN

MacIntyre

• This hunting tartan (top right) is a very popular MacIntyre tartan.

• The MacIntyres descended from Muriach the Wright – their Gaelic name, Mac-an tsaoir, means 'son of the wright'.

MacIntyre ancestry is very ancient. Scots folk songs tell of the Clan MacIntyre on the Island of Skye as early as 800 AD. Three centuries later, they settled at Glen Noe by Ben Cruachan on the shores of Loch Etive in Argyllshire. Later, in 1470, this became Clan Campbell territory, after which the MacIntyres were faced with paying the Campbells a land rent. From the 12th century, the MacIntyres served as hereditary foresters, first to the Clan MacDougall, later to the Stewarts of Lorn. They also had many other talents. The Cladich MacIntyres became known for weaving hose and garters. One of Scotland's premier Gaelic poets was Duncan MacIntyre, who was imprisoned for writing a poem criticizing the banning of Highland dress after the Jacobite rebellion in 1745.

ANCIENT MACINTYRE HUNTING TARTAN

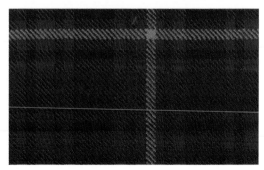

MODERN MACINTYRE TARTAN

MacIvor

• Lacking a hunting tartan themselves, the MacIvers wear the MacArthur hunting tartan.

• The Clan MacIver, whose forbears were Vikings, were associated with Clan Campbell.

The name MacIver came from Iver Crom, who received lands at Asknish, Lergachonzie and Glassary in Cowal from Alexander II after fighting for him against Viking invaders. The MacIvers served the Earls of Argyll and were rewarded for their loyalty in 1564, when the 5th Earl recognized them as a clan distinct from the Campbells. Unfortunately, in 1685, the MacIvers supported Archibald, 9th Earl of Argyll, against the Catholic King James VII (of Scotland) and II (of England and Ireland), and their lands became forfeit. Although they were restored in 1689, the clan was demoted and had to assume the arms and name of Clan Campbell once again.

MODERN MACIVOR TARTAN

MacKay

• Except for its colour, which is dark green, the McKay tartan is very similar to the Gunn tartan, suggesting proximity between their clan territories.

• Once known by the names Morgan and Aiodh, the MacKays were a powerful clan descended from the old Scots royal house of MacEth.

The MacKay chief, Angus Dubh, and his clan were defeated when Donald, 2nd Lord of the Isles, invaded Sutherland. Angus was imprisoned, but subsequently, he and his captor became reconciled. So much so that Angus married Donald's sister, a grand daughter of King Robert III. and was subsequently granted lands by his brother-in-law. The MacKays' power base was at Strathnaver, in northwest Scotland, but these lands were sold in 1642 and other McKay territory was purchased in 1829 by the Sutherland family.

ANCIENT MACKAY TARTAN

MacKellar

• The Clan MacKellar is a sept of the Clan Campbell.

• From the 13th century, the chief concentration of MacKellars was in Argyll.

The MacKellars derive their name either from a French saint, Hilary, who lived in the 4th century, or from Hilarius, Bishop of Poitiers in France in 1230. In Gaelic, their name is Mac Ealair, meaning 'son of Hilary'. The name retained the form of Hilary or Hilarius for some time, and is printed this way in several early documents. The first MacKellar to make an appearance in the ancient records was Patrick MacKellar, who witnessed a charter at Carnasseriein 1436. Some years later, in 1488, the name of Archibald Makelar of Argyll, described as a 'Scottyshman', appeared on a document awarding him safe conduct to England.

MODERN MACKELLAR TARTAN

WEATHERED MACKELLAR TARTAN

MacKenzie

• The MacKenzie tartan, a variation on the Black Watch tartan, is also worn by the regiment of the Seaforth Highlanders, which was raised in 1778.

• This tartan is also worn by the Highland Light Infantry raised in 1777 by Lord MacLeod, heir to the MacKenzie earls of Cromarty.

MacKenzie is a Celtic name, Maccoinneach, which means Son of the Bright One, or Son of Kenneth. Mackenzie clan lands were sited in Ross-shire and around Muir of Ord until the 12th century, when the Mackenzies relocated to Western Ross, in Kintail. By 1267, the MacKenzies had occupied Eilean Donan castle, at the mouth of Loch Duich and soon after acquired the lands of Kintail. These lands became a barony in 1508, and in 1609 Kenneth, 12th chief of the Mackenzie clan, became Lord Kintail. Two earldoms (Seaforth and Cromarty) followed in 1623 and 1702. The clan's followers, the Macraes, became bodyguards to the Mackenzie chiefs, and the MacLennons acted as their hereditary standard bearers.

MODERN MACKENZIE TARTAN

ANCIENT MACKENZIE TARTAN

MacKinlay

• The MacKinlay tartan, first recorded in 1906, has been described as 'Black Watch with red'.

• The Livingstones have been named as the most likely progenitors of the MacKinlays.

The Clan MacKinlay were based in the Lennox district, where their main sept was described in 1723 as being descended from Buchanan of Drumikill. The clan name is believed to come from MacFhionnlaigh or 'Son of Finlay Mor'. The Clan Farquharson of Braemar appear to have a better claim to this particular ancestor, who was the royal standard bearer at the battle of Pinkie in 1547. In common with several others clans in Lennox, the MacKinlays probably emigrated to Ireland when the English 'plantations' were being established there in the 17th century. Their descendants were the MacKinlays and MacGinlays of Ireland.

ANCIENT MACKINLAY TARTAN

MacKinnon

• The earliest known date for the MacKinnon tartan is 1816, though there have been several variations in its colours.

• The MacKinnons claim descent from Kenneth Mac Alpin, through his great-grandson Fingon.

Their ancestral lands centred around Mull and Skye, where they were probably vassals of the Lords of the Isles. The MacKinnons supported the Stewart monarchy, fighting on the royalist side at the battle of Inverlochy in 1645 during the civil war, and at the battle of Worcester in 1651. They again supported the Stewarts in both Jacobite rebellions, of 1715 and 1745. However, the aged McKinnon chief was imprisoned in London after Culloden and did not return to Scotland until 1747. In his absence, the MacKinnon lands, held by the clan for 400 years, had been sold off.

MODERN MACKINNON TARTAN

Mackintosh

• The Mackintosh tartan, first known in 1815 and first recorded in 1831, was listed by Wilson of Bannockburn as the 'Caledonian sett'.

• The Mackintosh chiefs were also chiefs of Clan Chattan.

Mackintosh is an anglicized version of the Gaelic name Mac an toisich (*toisich* meaning 'chief' or 'leader'). The Mackintoshes were descended from the ancient royal house of Dalriada and their lands stretched from Petty to Lochaber. The lands of Petty came to the Mackintosh clan after the first chief, Shaw (son of Duncan MacDuff, Earl of Fife), helped King Malcolm IV suppress a revolt in Morayshire in 1160. The clan chiefs were among the most dominant in Scotland. The Mackintoshes conducted vicious feuds against the Gordons, the MacDonnells of Keppoch, the Camerons and the Comyns. The Mackintoshes were loyal to the Stewarts in the civil wars and both Jacobite rebellions. As punishment, many Mackintosh clansmen were transported to America.

MODERN MACKINTOSH TARTAN

ANCIENT MACKINTOSH TARTAN

MacLachlan

• The earliest known date for the MacLachlan tartan is 1831.

• This tartan was one of three district versions of the MacLachlan sett and is the one woven today.

Lachlan Mor, ancestor of the ancient MacLachlan clan, gave his name to several places around Loch Fyne, including the barony of Strathlachlan and Castle Lachlan. Traditionally, Lachlan Mor, and therefore the MacLachlans, were descended from the Irish Ui Niell kings. Gillespie MacLachlan supported Robert the Bruce and sat in his first Parliament of 1308. Later McLachlans fought in both the Jacobite rebellions. The clan chief was killed at Culloden in 1746 and the MacKinnon estates became forfeit for three years. The MacLachlans forged several unions by marriage with the powerful Clan Campbell, and although they also married into the Clan Lamont, they and the Lamonts often indulged in violent feuds. This reached a bloody peak in 1646, when the Campbells and MacLachlans combined to massacre the Lamonts.

MODERN MACLACHLAN TARTAN

ANCIENT MACLACHLAN TARTAN

123

MacLaine of Lochbuie

• The MacLaine of Lochbuie tartan was first recorded c.1810-1820.

• The 13th-century warrior Gillean of the Battleaxe was the ancestor of the MacLaines of Lochbuie.

The first MacLaine of Lochbuie chief was Reaganach, or Hector the Stern, who received lands in Mull from the Lord of the Isles in 1350. Through Gillean, the Lochbuie clan may originate from the ancient kings of Dalriada. So do the MacLeans, who split from Lochbuie after an argument over the leadership. This led to vicious feuding and after 1494, John Og of Lochbuie and two of his sons were killed by the MacLeans of Duart at Lochbuie castle. A third son, the infant Murdoch, was smuggled to Ireland for safety. On reaching manhood, Murdoch returned and recaptured the castle.

MODERN MACLAINE OF LOCHBUIE TARTAN

MacLaren

• The MacLaren tartan dates from before 1820 and was once called the Regent tartan after the Prince Regent.

• The name Regent tartan lapsed after 1820, when the Prince succeeded to the throne as King George IV.

Traditionally, Lord, son of Erc, who landed in Argyll in 503AD, was the ancestor of the MacLarens. By the 12th century, the McLarens held land in Balquhidder and Strathearn. Although the earldom was taken over by King Robert II in 1344, the clan remained loyal to the Stewart royal family and fought for them in several wars and battles. This included the Jacobite rebellion of 1745, when many MacLarens died at Culloden. The MacLarens were also involved in several feuds and suffered heavy casualties in a raid by the MacGregors of Glendochart in 1558.

ANCIENT MACLAREN TARTAN

MacLean of Duart

• The MacLean of Duart tartan is similar to the Royal Stewart, except that the number of threads and colours have been reversed.

• Sir Fitzroy MacLean, 25th chief and 10th baronet, lived to be 101 years old.

The MacLeans and MacLaines were descended from two brothers, whose ancestor was Gillean of the Battleaxe. One of them, Lachlan Lubanach, was the progenitor of the MacLeans of Duart. The MacLeans were supporters of the MacDougalls of Lorn, but later switched loyalty to the MacDonalds of the Isles and ranked among their most powerful vassalls. Later, though, the MacLeans rose to become one of the most important clans in the Western Isles. They fought bravely for the Stewarts, including seven brothers who died while protecting their chief at the battle of Inverkeithing in 1651.

WEATHERED MACLEAN OF DUART TARTAN

MacLellan

• The Gaelic name Macgille Fhaolain is the origin of MacLellan. The name means son of the servant of St. Filan.

• MacLellans were legendary fighting men.

In 15th-century Galloway, there were records of 14 knights named MacLellan, although their activities were not always particularly chivalrous. Sir Patrick MacLellan of Bombie did such damage to Clan Douglas territory that he had to forfeit his estates as punishment. They were retrieved by Sir Patrick's son after he killed a gypsy, spiked his head on his sword and presented it to King James II. The feud with the Clan Douglas was by no means at an end. In the 15th century, according to tradition, the MacLellans brought the giant gun Mons Meg to Threave, the Douglas castle, and used it to batter down the walls.

ANCIENT MACLELLAN TARTAN

127

MacLeod

• The original source for the Macleod tartan was the tartan used by John Mackenzie, Lord MacLeod, when raising his Highlanders Regiment in 1777.

• The MacLeod of Harris tartan is sometimes called the Hunting MacLeod.

MACLEOD TARTAN

Tormod was progenitor of the MacLeods of Glenelg, Harris and Dunvegan. The MacLeods of Lewis, Waternish, Assynt and Raasay descend from Torquil, son of Viking Olave the Black. The first leader of the MacLeods of Raasay was Rough Malcolm, brother of Ruari MacLeod, 10th chief of the MacLeods of Lewis. The Macleods were almost annihilated fighting for the future Stewart King Charles II at Worcester in 1651. The most renowned leader of the Harris MacLeods was Roderick, the 16th chief, better known as Rory Mor, who was knighted in 1603 by the Stuart King James VI (of Scotland) and I (of England and Ireland).

MODERN MACLEOD OF HARRIS TARTAN

Macmillan

• This Macmillan tartan, called 'ancient', was first recorded in 1847, when it was described by James Logan as 'identical' with the Buchanan tartan.

• The Macmillans, whose name means 'son of the tonsured one', may have been descended from Celtic priests.

The ancestor of the Clan Macmillan, Gilchrist, whose name meant 'servant of Christ', was the son of Cormac, a 12th-century Bishop of Dunkeld. Although the Macmillans settled in Galloway, Badokenan on Loch Fyne and in Glens Shera and Shira, their main powerbase was at Lochaber and Knapdale. The clan obtained their feudal grant of Knap from the Lord of the Isles in the 16th century. He permitted them to hold it 'so long as the wave beats on the rock', doubtless a poetic way of saying that it should be theirs permanently.

ANCIENT MACMILLAN TARTAN

MacNab

• The MacNab tartan has an identical structure to the Black Watch, but with colours changed – crimson in place of black, green for blue and scarlet for green.

• The Clan MacNab is another branch of the Siol Alpine.

The MacNabs claim descent from the abbots of Glendochart in Perthshire, where their chief lands were located for many centuries. However, except for the barony of Bovain in Glendochart, the lands were lost after 1314, when the MacNabs opposed Robert the Bruce. Subsequent MacNabs were supporters of the Stewart monarchy, both in the civil wars and at the battle of Worcester in 1651, where their chief was killed. In the Jacobite rebellion of 1745, though, loyalties were divided: the clan was for Bonnie Prince Charlie, while their chief was against him.

MODERN MACNAB TARTAN

MacNaughten

• The MacNaughten tartan is closely related to the MacDuff and was first recorded in 1831.

• The ancestor of the Clan MacNaughten was the Pictish King of Moray Nechtan or Nauchten, who founded Abernethy.

The MacNaughten lands were situated along the shore of Loch Awe in Lorn. In 1267, King Alexander III gave Gilchrist MacNaughten custody of the island and castle of Fraoch Eilean on Awe. The clan opposed Robert the Bruce, but later pledged loyalty to his descendants, the royal Stewarts. Alexander MacNaughten, who raised a band of archers to fight for Charles I in the civil war, became one of Charles II's courtiers and also supported King James VII (of Scotland) and II (of England and Ireland). In 1689, after James was forced into exile, he praised the MacNaughtens for their loyalty.

WEATHERED MACNAUGHTEN TARTAN

131

MacNeill

• The MacNeill clan tartan was known in 1819, but was not recorded until 1886.

• Among the many variants of the MacNeill tartan is the MacNeill of Colonsay sett, which has the same scheme as the Graham of Montrose tartan.

The MacNeills are another clan with ancient Celtic origins, claiming their ancestry from the Ui Neill dynasty of Ireland and a legendary forbear, Niall of the Nine Hostages. The MacNeills first came to Scotland when Aodh O'Neill crossed the Irish sea in 1049 and landed on the Hebridean island of Barra. The area later became the heartland of the McNeills. The clan were vassals of the Lords of the Isles, who, in 1427, gave Gilleonan O'Neill Barra and Boisdale in South Uist. Some two centuries later, the MacNeills acquired the island of Colonsay after the original inhabitants, the MacFies, were dispossessed by the MacDonalds. The MacNeills seem to have been a riotous lot. Until his capture in 1610, the 15th MacNiell chief, Ruari, was a pirate operating out of his fortress on Kisimul.

ANCIENT MACNEILL OF BARRA TARTAN

MODERN MACNEILL OF COLONSAY TARTAN

MacPhail

• The MacPhail tartan shown comes from the Scottish Tartans Society archives and is dated between 1930 and 1950.

• Paul MacPhail, the ancestor of the Clan McPhail, lived at Invernarnie, near Nairn in the 15th century.

The MacPhail surname, first recorded in 1414, came from the Gaelic for 'son of Paul'. The Clan McPhail had ties to the Camerons, the Mackintoshes and the MacKays, and in about 1500, came under the protection of the Clan Chattan confederation. Later McPhail chiefs chose wives from the Shaw family of Tordarroch and also from the Clan Chattan. McPhails joined the 1715 rebellion as officers in the Chattan regiment, and after the defeat the chief's heir was among those clansmen transported to America. He died on board ship.

MODERN MACPHAIL TARTAN

MacPherson

• Before 1822, the MacPherson tartan was called 'Kidd and Caledonian' in the Wilson of Bannockburn pattern book.

• Like the Macmillans and the MacNabs, the MacPhersons have clerical origins.

MacPherson means 'son of the parson' – that is, Muireach Cattenach, parson of Badenoch (later the MacPherson heartland). Muireach was also captain of Clan Chattan. Of all the MacPhersons in Inverness-shire, the family of Cluny was the most senior. The MacPhersons were keen supporters of the royal Stewarts in the 17th-century civil war and the 1745 rebellion. Ewen MacPherson of Cluny brought 600 clansmen to the aid of Bonnie Prince Charlie, and later helped him escape capture by the Hanoverian forces. As punishment, his house was burned and he was a fugitive for the next nine years.

MODERN MACPHERSON TARTAN

MacQuarrie

• This is the most common variant of the MacQuarrie tartan and is related to the red MacDonald tartan.

• Although only a small clan, the MacQuarries have eight tartans in the Scottish Tartans Society archives.

The MacQuarries are descended from Guiaire, brother of Fingon, progenitor of the MacKinnons. The first known MacQuarrie chief, Iain of Ulva, died around 1473. The MacQuarries followed the Lords of the Isles, but after 1493 transferred alliegance to the MacLeans of Duart. With them, they supported the Stewarts in the civil wars and at Inverkeithing in 1651, where John MacQuarrie of Ulva was killed, together with most of the clansmen. MacQuarrie lands were not lost as a result, but by around 1800, the clan was so in debt that it was forced to sell out.

MODERN MACQUARRIE TARTAN

MacQueen

• This tartan, now of Clan MacQueen, was originally called Revan, after Revan MacMulmor MacAngus MacQueen.

• MacQueen, a Celtic name, was a variant of 'Macsween' or 'son of Sweyn'.

The MacQueens claimed common descent with the MacDonalds and also kinship with the High Kings of Ireland. In the 15th century, MacQueens provided an escort, led by Revan MacMulmor MacAngus MacQueen, for the Clanranald bride of a Mackintosh chief. Consequently, they became known as Clan Revan. The MacQueens were members of the Clan Chattan federation. Their main branch became Lairds of Corriborough, but the family later went into decline. The clan chiefs are said to have emigrated to New Zealand, while other MacQuarries scattered throughout the English-speaking world.

MODERN MACQUEEN TARTAN

MacRae

• The Clan MacRae has 18 tartans listed in the archives of the Scottish Tartans society.

• The surname MacRae means 'son of grace' in Gaelic, suggesting origins in the clergy.

The Clan MacRae was mainly centred at Kintail, on Loch Duich, where they were apparently established by Fionnla Dubh Macgillechriosd, who died in 1416. The Macraes were, at first, vassals of the Earls of Ross but later followed the Mackenzies. Another branch of the clan, the Macraes of Conchra were established in 1677 by Alexander, son of the Reverend John MacRae of Dingwall. Over time, various Macraes served as constables of Eilean Donan castle and chamberlains and vicars of Kintail. The famous Fernaig Manuscript of 1688–1693, an important contribution to Gaelic literature, was compiled by the poet Duncan MacRae.

ANCIENT MACRAE HUNTING TARTAN

137

MacTaggert

• As a sept of Clan Ross, the Ross tartan is listed as the appropriate sett for the Clan MacTaggert.

• In 1583, three MacTaggerts were accused of arson; and in 1588, Catherine MacTaggert was charged with being a witch.

MacTaggert is taken from Mac an t'sagairt, meaning 'son of a priest'. The first record of the name was in 1215, when King Alexander II knighted one Ferquhard Macintaggert, whose name meant the 'son of the red priest of Applecross'. This was Macintaggert's reward for suppressing a rebellion against the king and executing its leaders. Afterwards, Macintaggert presented King Alexander with their severed heads, a recognized way of claiming credit for an enterprising deed. However, an even more dazzling reward was in store for Macintaggert: the earldom of Ross.

ANCIENT MACTAGGERT TARTAN

MacTavish

• The traditional MacTavish lands at Dunardarie came to the clan by means of a 14th-century charter.

• The MacTavishes have links with several other Scots clans, including the mighty Mackintoshes

The Clan MacTavish, whose name comes from MacTamhais, son of Tammas or Thomas, is regarded as a sept of the Clan Campbell. However, one branch, the MacTavishes of Stratherrick, are linked closely to the Clan Fraser. The MacTavishes are believed to be descended from Tavis Corr, who was the natural son of Gillespick. They were valiant supporters of the Jacobite cause, and fought in both the 1715 and 1745 rebellions. However, in 1745, they lacked their chief, who had been imprisoned by the Duke of Argyll, and so took part in the rebellion under the aegis of Clan Mackintosh.

MODERN MACTAVISH TARTAN

MacThomas

• The tartan shown was adopted officially by the MacThomas society in 1975.

• At Glenshee, in the Grampian Mountains, the clan was known as the MacComie, but this changed to MacThomas in the 17th century.

Tomaidh, or Thomas, Mor, who gave Clan MacThomas its name, was descended from a grandson of William Mackintosh, 8th Chief of Clan Chattan. The clan centre was Thom, on the East Bank of Sheerwater, but this changed in 1600, when Robert MacComie, the 4th Chief, was murdered. His brother, John MacComie of Finegand, replaced him and made Finegand, in Glenshee, his principal seat. Another John MacComie, the 7th Chief, resented tax collectors. He once hired an Italian hit man to deal with them, but the next taxman proved the handier swordsman, and killed the Italian.

ANCIENT MACTHOMAS TARTAN

Marshall

• **This tartan is called the Keith, Austin and Marshall. The Marshalls were a sept of Clan Keith, hereditary Great Marischals of Scotland.**

• *Maréchal*, **the French word from which the name Marshall was derived, meant 'horse servant' – either a blacksmith or a farrier.**

The title Marshal came to Britain after 1066 and its holders soon became prestigious royal officers. As a surname, the earliest record appeared in 1084, when Goisfridus Marescal was named in the Gold Roll of the Domesday Book. In Scotland, after 1136, Maledoni Marescal was the first among several officials with similar surnames to put their signatures to charters and legal documents. Although the Marshalls are regarded as a sept of Clan Keith, the surname itself did not come into use until late in the 17th century.

MODERN MARSHALL TARTAN

Matheson

• **The Matheson tartan was first recorded in 1850.**

• **The Clan Matheson, whose name means 'son of the bear', once held lands at Lochalsh and Kintail.**

One clan chief, Cormac MacMathan, earned praise from the Earl of Ross for his courage fighting against the Vikings who invaded Scotland in the late 13th century. The power of the Mathesons had become quite formidable by the 15th century: in 1427, it was said that the clan chief had 2000 men at his disposal, which made the Mathesons as mighty as the MacKenzies. In the 16th century, Matheson power and influence went into decline. Some Mathesons established themselves at Bennetsfield in the Black Isle, where Murchadha Buidhe, or Murdoch, settled in the 17th century. The present chiefs of the Bennetsfield Mathesons are Murdoch's descendants. Other Mathesons set up home in Sutherland, but this branch was decimated by the Highland Clearances of 1763–75. By the early 19th century, almost all of the Matheson lands in Scotland had been lost.

MODERN MATHESON HUNTING TARTAN

ANCIENT MATHESON HUNTING TARTAN

Maxwell

• The Clan Maxwell tartan dates back for 1842, when it was included in the *Vestiarium Scoticum*.

• A fishery called Maccus' Wiel – Maccus' whirlpool – was the origin of the name Maxwell.

Maccus, a Saxon lord, received land – and the fishery – by the River Tweed from King David I around 1150. His descendants soon became prestigious. Maccus' grandsons, John and Aymer Maccuswell, were Chamberlains of Scotland. After 1424, the Maxwells and the Johnstons shared the wardenship of the Western Marches and this led to a feud. In 1593, the 7th Lord Maxwell was killed in a battle with the Johnstons near Lockerbie. A later Maxwell, William, 5th Earl of Nithsdale and a Jacobite supporter, staged a spectacular escape from the Tower of London after being sentenced to death for treason in 1715.

MODERN MAXWELL TARTAN

Melville

• The Melville tartan, called the Oliphant and Melville, dates from 1848.

• Guillaume de Malaville – William Melville – was reputedly a commander at the battle of Hastings.

Malaville in Normandy was the origin of the surname Melville. In 1124, de Malavilles went to Scotland with King David I and received a grant of lands in Midlothian, outside Edinburgh. Melvilles became keepers of the royal castles and royal ambassadors or, while Sir John Melville of Raith became a favourite of James V, who gave him the lands of Murdocairnie in Fife. Sir Robert Melville, royal ambassador and Vice Chancellor, was created Baron Melville in 1616. The 4th Baron Melville served King William III and Queen Mary II as Secretary of State for Scotland and was also created 1st Earl of Melville.

ANCIENT OLIPHANT AND MELVILLE TARTAN

Menzies

• This red and green hunting tartan (top right) was first known in 1815, but not recorded until 1893.

• The black-and-white coloured Menzies tartan (bottom right) is a dress tartan.

The Menzies originate from Mesnières in Normandy: the name became 'Manners' in England, and in Scotland, de Menzies (pronounced 'Mingis'). The family rose to prominence in royal government circles. In 1249, Sir Robert de Menzies became chamberlain to King Alexander II, and with his son he was granted the lands of Glen Lyon, Atholl, Rannoch and Weem in Strathtay, where Menzies Castle was later built, in 1488. Sir Robert Menzies was a supporter of Robert the Bruce in the wars of Scots independence and was further rewarded with lands in Glendochart, Finlarig, Glenorchy and Durisdeer. Being major landowners brought the clan into conflict with the neighbouring Campbells and Stewarts of Garth. The Menzies supported the royal Stewart cause in the 17th-century civil wars and, later, in the two Jacobite rebellions.

MENZIES HUNTING TARTAN

MENZIES DRESS TARTAN

Middleton

• The Clan Middleton is believed to have taken its name from the lands of Middleton near Laurencekirk, Kincardineshire.

• General John Middleton fought on both sides in the 17th-century civil war.

John Middleton, son of Middleton of Coldham, was a professional soldier. In the civil wars, he first defeated the Marquis of Montrose and forced him into exile, but later he could not bring himself to surrender King Charles I to the army of Parliament. In 1648, Middleton attempted to rescue the imprisoned monarch, but failed. Afterwards, he fought for Charles' son and heir at Worcester in 1651 and was made Earl of Middleton in 1660. The line did not last long: it became forfeit in the 18th century after Charles, 2nd Earl of Middleton supported the Jacobite rebellions.

MODERN MIDDLETON TARTAN

Mitchell

• The Mitchell name was taken from Michel, the Norman French version of the Hebrew name Michael, which meant 'who is like God'.

• A Mitchell clansman was one of the signatories of the treaty of Berwick of 1354, by which King David II was freed from imprisonment by the English.

When the Michels arrived in Scotland some time after 1066, their name was pronounced with a guttural 'ch' as in 'loch'. In 1489, one John Michell held Dumbarton Castle and was rewarded with lands in Ayrshire and Stirling. For some time, the 't' in Mitchell was omitted from the name, but it was used by the Mitchells of Craigends by the early 18th century. In 1719, 'Mitchell' became official when Alexander Mitchell registered a coat of arms as 'Mitchell of Mitchell'.

ANCIENT MITCHELL TARTAN

Moffat

• In 1983, the Moffats acquired a clan chief, Francis Moffat, for the first time since 1563. This event was celebrated by the creation of the special tartan shown here.

• The Moffats were probably Viking in origin, descending from a daughter of Andlaw, who came to Scotland from Norway during the 10th century.

Andlaw's youngest daughter married William, the progenitor of the Movats, whose name developed into Moffat. By the 13th century, the Moffats were important lairds in Scotland, holding lands that included Corehead, Ericstane, Meikleholmside, Braefoot, Newton, Gardenholm and the barony of Eskdale. However, mounting debt forced the gradual sale of these territories and by the early 17th century, the clan was landless. They remained so until 1920, when the clan acquired Craigbeck and Garrowgill.

MODERN MOFFAT TARTAN

Montgomery

• This Montgomery family tartan was first recorded in 1893, though it may date from 1707.

• The Montgomerys were Norman by origin, taking their name from the castle of Sainte Foy de Montgomery at Lisieux.

Roger de Mundegumbrie, a distant cousin of William the Conqueror, joined the invading force, apparently commanding the Norman vanguard at Hastings. In Scotland, the first Montgomery on record was Robert, who acquired the lands of Eaglesham in Renfrewshire after 1165. The family was ennobled around 1448, when Alexander Montgomery became 1st Lord Montgomery, and acquired the earldom of Eglinton around 1508. In a feud with the Cunninghams of Glencairn, the Montgomerys killed every Cunningham they could find to avenge the 4th Earl of Eglinton's murder.

MODERN MONTGOMERY TARTAN

Morgan

• The presence of a Clan Morgan in Scotland was first noted in the *Book of Deer*, which was written at an unknown, but probably quite early, date.

• The evidence of the *Book of Deer* suggests that the Morgans lived in Aberdeenshire.

The Morgans were also in the Sutherlands where, later, the MacKays were known as 'Clan Morgan'. Subsequently, the Morgans were classed as a sept of Clan MacKay. The name Morgan, meaning 'sea-born' or 'bright', may be Celtic.

The *Book of Deer* emphasizes the antiquity of the family, describing how their ancestors made sacrifices to their pagan gods as well as to Christian saints. Dual religious practices like this were common in the very early stage of conversion to Christianity, which began in Scotland around the end of the 4th century AD.

MODERN MORGAN TARTAN

Morrison

• The pattern of this Morrison tartan was taken from the covering of an old family bible.

• The Clan Morrison comprises three separate families, each of a different origin.

One branch of the Morrisons descends from a Viking, Ghille Mhuire – 'servant of the Virgin Mary' – who was shipwrecked with his crew on the shore of Lewis. They saved themselves by clinging to driftwood: this is why driftwood is a feature of the Morrison clan badge. His descendants were later counted among the most ancient clans on Lewis and some of them, it appears, held the hereditary office of brieve or judge. Other Morrisons are descended from Irish bards who emigrated to the Hebrides. There were also Morrisons in Aberdeenshire, who had Norman origins. Their Norman ancestor was named Mauricius, meaning 'swarthy'.

MODERN MORRISON TARTAN

Mowat

• The Clan Mowat originated in Normandy and settled in Wales and Scotland.

• In about 1259, Bernhard de Mohane, or Mowat, was one of the nobles who concluded a treaty between Scotland and Wales.

The Mowat's original name was Monhault, or Montealt, meaning 'high mountain'. Some Mowats became Lords of the Welsh Marches; others went to Scotland, where Sir William Montealt acquired the Lordship of Ferne in Forfarshire from King William the Lion. Mowats were frequent signatories to grants, agreements, letters and other documents, though the name varied: Monte Alto, Mouat, and de Mowat were all used. In the 14th century, the Mowats received a charter, from Robert the Bruce, for Freswick in Caithness and were classed at that time as the principal family in Bucholly, Aberdeenshire.

MODERN MOWAT TARTAN

Muir

• The earliest known date for the Muir tartan was 1880, although it was not first recorded until 1930.

• The Lowland meaning of Muir is 'large' or 'big', whereas the Highland form comes from Middle English for a low, grassy hill.

The principal Muir family, who spelled their name 'Mure', lived at Rowallan in Ayrshire. Mure was among the noble names appearing in the Ragman Rolls of 1296, and in the 14th century David II knighted Sir William Mure, who gave his sons as hostage for the king's ransom. In 1346, Sir William's grand-daughter Elizabeth married the future King Robert II and became the mother of king Robert III. The Mures were solidly loyal to the Stewart royal family, and many died with King James IV at Flodden in 1513.

MODERN MUIR TARTAN

Munro

• In early versions of this Munro tartan, around 1810, the crimson was replaced by bright pink.

• The Munros used the Black Watch as their hunting tartan.

The first Munro, Hugh of Foulis, probably lived on Easter Ross and died in 1126. Easter Ross has long been the Munros' home, and in the early 13th century, George Munro of Foulis held a charter for the territory from the Earl of Sutherland. Robert Munro, then clan chief, fought for Robert the Bruce at Bannockburn. Later, the Munros forged their own royal connection when Robert Munro married a niece of King Robert II's queen, Euphemia. Munros made their mark on American history. Ebenezer Munro apparently fired the first shot in the American Revolution, and in 1816 James Monroe became fifth US President.

MODERN MUNRO TARTAN

Murrays

• The Murray of Atholl tartan (top right) is based on the Black Watch pattern.

• The first Murray to adopt the Tullibardine tartan (bottom right) was Charles, 1st Earl of Dunmore, second son of the 1st Marquis of Tullibardine.

The Murray clan was established in Moray in the 12th century, when their ancestor, Freskin, received lands from King David I. Later, the Murrays founded other branches, mainly at Tullibardine in 1282 and at Atholl where their estates came to them on the marriage in 1629 of William, 2nd Earl of Tullibardine to the heiress of the 5th Earl of Atholl. The Murrays became important in Scots national affairs. Sir Andrew Murray, Freskin's grandson, supported William Wallace and after the death of King Robert the Bruce in 1329, he became Regent of Scotland. The Murrays of Tallibardine acquired a barony in 1443. Sir William Murray, who inherited the estates in 1446, was sheriff of Perthshire. By the 16th century, the chieftainship had been claimed by the Tullibardine Murrays.

MODERN MURRAY OF ATHOLL TARTAN

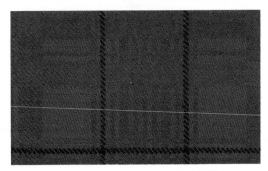

ANCIENT MURRAY OF TULLIBARDINE TARTAN

Napier

• The Napier tartan has been called a blend of elaborate Shepherd plaid and a true tartan.

• The Napiers may have served as naperers, caring for the royal linen.

The Clan Napier was traditionally descended from ancient Celtic royalty through the Earls of Lennox. Napiers first appeared around 1290, with a grant to John de Napier from Malcolm, Earl of Lennox of lands at Kilmahew in Dunbartonshire, which the family retained for over 500 years. Napiers were often found in royal service. In 1440, Alexander Napier was appointed Comptroller of the Royal Household to James II. Archibald Napier, son of John, the 7th Laird of Merchiston – the same John Napier who invented logarithms – attended King James VI on his journey to London after he became James I of England and Ireland in 1603.

MODERN NAPIER TARTAN

Nicolson/MacNicol

• The Nicolson tartan was first recognized around 1845, but was not recorded until 1950.

• The Nicolsons and the MacNicols officially became separate clans in 1980.

In the Highlands of Scotland, the name is MacNicol; in the Lowlands, it is Nicolson. Both may derive from the surname of a Viking general, Anders Nicolassen, who may have settled in Scotland.

In 1263, Nicolassen, one of the chief barons of King Haakon of Norway, commanded the Norwegian army at the battle of Largs, in which his forces suffered a heavy defeat. Nicolassen returned to Scotland in 1266 to negotiate the Treaty of Perth, which finally handed sovereignty of the contested Scots islands to the Scots kings. Subsequently, it appears, he decided to settle in Scotland, and founded a clan which became the clan Nicolson.

MODERN NICHOLSON TARTAN

Nisbet

• The Nisbet tartan appeared in the *Vestiarium Scoticum* of 1842, where it was described as 'Mackintosh'.

• The tartan has considerable similarity to the Dunbar tartan.

The lands of Nisbet near Edrom in Berwickshire probably included a nose-shaped hill or bend that gave its name to the territory, and after that to the barony and the family which held the title. The Nisbet family was well founded, and by the 13th century they had witnessed several charters and held high posts at court and the church. In addition, the Nisbets gave exemplary service to the Scots kings, first in defence of the southern borders of Scotland during the reign of King David II in the 14th century, and then in the 17th-century civil wars between Charles I and Parliament.

MODERN NISBET TARTAN

Ogilvie

• The Ogilvie tartan shown top right, also known as Drummond of Strathallen, is regarded as one of the most complex of all tartans.

• The Ogilvie hunting tartan shown bottom right was called 'Ogilvy of Inverquharity' in the *Vestiarium Scoticum* of 1842.

In about 1163, King William the Lion granted the barony of Ogilvie to a descendant of the ancient Celtic earls of Angus. Twelve years later, Gillebride, founder of the clan, gave his lands to his son Gilbert. The Ogilvies acquired Cortachy and Airlie and in 1491, Sir James Ogilvie was created Lord of Airlie. The lordship became an earldom in 1639. During the 17th-century civil war, James, the 2nd Earl of Airlie was captured but escaped from the Castle of St. Andrews the night before he was due to be executed.

ANCIENT OGILVIE TARTAN

ANCIENT OGILVIE HUNTING TARTAN

Oliphant

• This tartan is also known as the Oliphant and Melville: the Clan Melville tartan has a similar pattern.

• The Oliphant clan descended from the de Olifards, who were Norman adventurers.

David de Olifard's link to Scotland began when he saved King David I's life during a siege. He went on to become the forbear of the Clan Oliphant and in 1458, his descendant Lawrence received the title of Lord Oliphant. One of Lawrence's sons, William, founded the Oliphants of Gask and another, George, founded the Oliphants of Bachilton. The family were fervent nationalists: in 1320, Sir William Oliphant signed the Declaration of Arbroath, which proclaimed Scots independence from England. In 1745, Laurence Oliphant of Gask and his eldest son were attainted for their part in the Jacobite rebellion.

ANCIENT OLIPHANT TARTAN

Oliver

• Both the tartans shown were designed for the Clan Oliver Society.

• The tartan shown, top right, is based on 'Tweedside', a cottage weavers' formula of around 1820. The tartan shown, bottom right, is based on the Tweedside District sett of around 1820.

The French name Olivier, a maker or seller of olive oil, may be the origin of the name Oliver, suggesting the family came to Britain from Normandy. There are reputed links with the Frasers, who also came from Normandy, but the arrival of two families in Scotland seems unconnected. The first recorded Oliver was Walter Olifer, who witnessed the royal gift of a serf to the Bishop of Glasgow in 1180. Ultimately, the Clan Oliver became a strong force in the Scots Borders, but suffered greatly from English raiders.

OLIVER HUNTING TARTAN

OLIVER TARTAN

Ramsay

• The tartan was first recorded in 1842, and may be connected to the Rob Roy MacGregor tartan.

• When the MacGregors were proscribed, they adopted the name Ramsay and possibly the Ramsay tartan as well.

The Ramsays came originally from Normandy and arrived in Scotland after entering the service of King David I. Sir Symon de Ramesie was later granted lands at Dalhousie in Midlothian. Afterwards, Ramsay signatures appear on many charters, including the Ragman Rolls of 1296, which was signed by Sir William de Ramsay. A little later, Sir William changed sides to support Robert the Bruce, and was a signatory in 1320 to the Declaration of Abroath, asserting Scots independence. After 1618, the Ramsays became earls of Dalhousie and after 1849, marquesses.

MODERN RAMSAY TARTAN

Rattray

• The Clan Rattray were followers, but not a sept, of the Murrays of Atholl.

• The ancient seat of the Rattrays is Draighall, Blairgowrie in Perthshire.

The barony of Rattray, which gave the clan its name, first came into their possession in the 11th century. The estate includes an archaeological gem, the ruins of the Pictish rath-tref, or fort dwelling, which was traditionally connected with ancient pagan rites. The Rattrays were influential and in 1315, Alexander Rattray was among the barons who decided the succession to the throne. The Rattrays were involved in a vicious feud with the earls of Atholl over the Fortinghall estates. In 1533, John Stewart, Earl of Atholl murdered the holder of the estates, Patrick Rattray, and threatened his successor, Silvester, to such an extent that he sought royal protection.

MODERN RATTRAY TARTAN

163

Robertson

WEATHERED ROBERTSON HUNTING TARTAN

• In around 1815, elders of Clan Robertson were unable to decide on the true Robertson tartan: as a result, Alexander Robertson of Struan adopted the Atholl tartan for his own use.

• The Robertson of Kindeace tartan, shown top right, is known as the Hunting Robertson, and was first recorded in 1810–20.

The very ancient Clan Robertson claimed descent from the royal house of Dunkeld, the Celtic mormaers (district rulers) and the Earls of Atholl. The clan's direct ancestor was Donnchadh Reamhar, or Duncan the Fat, but their name came from Robert Riach, or Grizzled Robert. He was the clan chief who, in 1437, captured the murderers of King James I and delivered them to the authorities for punishment. His reward, in 1451, was the Barony of Struan.

ANCIENT ROBERTSON TARTAN

Rose

• The clan Rose was first recorded in the *Vestiarium Scoticum* in 1842.

• The hunting tartan, top right, is similar to the Oliphant and Melville and to a tartan made for the New York Fire Department Pipe Band in 1966.

MODERN ROSE HUNTING TARTAN

The Clan Rose originated at Ros, near Caen, Normandy. In Scotland, they held the lands of Geddes in Inverness before the 13th century. The marriage of Hugh Rose to Mary, daughter of Sir Andrew de Bosco of Redcastle, brought the family lands at Kilravock on the Moray Firth. Kilravock became a barony in 1474. During the two Jacobite risings, the Clan Rose supported the Hanoverian dynasty. With their talent for diplomacy, they avoided the persistent and violent feuding common among other Scots clans and lived in remarkable harmony with their neighbours.

MODERN ROSE TARTAN

Ross

• **This tartan is the oldest and probably the most accurate version of the Ross tartan.**

• **Clan Ross was called Clann Andrias in Gaelic.**

The traditional ancestor of Clan Ross was Fearchar Mac-an-t-sagairt of Applecross in Wester Ross. The name Fearchar meant 'son of a priest'. In around 1215, Fearchar, who was already a substantial landowner and heir to the hereditary abbots of Applecross, earned himself a knighthood for helping King Alexander II put down a local revolt. After defeating the rebels in Moray, Fearchar had their heads cut off and stuffed into a bag which he presented to the King. Alexander subsequently created Fearchar Earl of Ross. Riding into war, the first earls of Ross would wear the sacred shirt of St Duthac for protection. This did not save the 4th Earl of Ross from being killed at the battle of Hallidon Hill against the English in 1333. Unfortunately, the family title ultimately became extinct in the 15th century.

MODERN ROSS TARTAN

ANCIENT ROSS HUNTING TARTAN

Russell

• The Russell tartan was called Galbraith in the Highland Society of London collection, Hunter in 1819 and 1824, and Russell in 1847.

• In 1987, the tartan was adopted by the US Air Force Reserve Pipe Band in honour of Billy Mitchell, 'father' of the US Air Force.

It seems likely that the Clan Russell had Norman origins and also that the early Russells had red hair, since the name probably comes from the Old French *rous*, meaning russet. Russell is also one of the earliest surviving Scots surnames and appeared on a charter for Paisley Abbey witnessed by Walter Russell in around 1164.

The Russells became landowners of some importance in Scotland, and after 1180, John Russel, son of Robert Russel of Duncanlaw, gave land for the foundation of a hospital.

ANCIENT RUSSELL TARTAN

MODERN RUSSELL TARTAN

Ruthven

• The Ruthven tartan was unnamed until it featured in the *Vestiarium Scoticum* of 1842.

• Although the Clan Ruthven is Norse in origin, their name comes from the Gaelic Ruadhainn, their lands in Perthshire.

The Ruthvens arrived in Perthshire during the 12th century. However, conspiracy ran in the family: in 1566, Patrick, 3rd Lord Ruthven, was one of the murderers of David Rizzio the secretary of Mary, Queen of Scots'. William, 4th Lord Ruthven, was created Earl of Gowrie in 1581, helped kidnap and imprison King James VI in 1582, and was executed for treason in 1584. In 1600, John, the 3rd Earl of Gowrie, lured James VI to his house in Perth and threatened to kill him, only to be himself killed by the King's attendants. After this, the Ruthven name was proscribed.

MODERN RUTHVEN TARTAN

Scott

• The tartan shown top right was first recorded after 1930 and became known as the Red Scott.

• The black-and-white Scott tartan, bottom right, was recorded in 1850 and was attributed to the novelist, Sir Walter Scott.

Clan Scott was among the mightiest of the Border clans. Its name derived from an ancient Celtic tribe, the Scotti, who arrived in Argyll from Ireland in around 500AD. The Scotti founded the kingdom of Dalriada, which expanded under the legendary 9th-century ruler Kenneth McAlpine into the kingdom and nation of Scotland. Two branches of the clan, the Scotts of Buccleuch and the Scotts of Balwearie, emerged after the 12th century. Subsequently, the Scotts of Buccleuch acquired a barony and in 1619, King James VI (of Scotland) and I (of England and Ireland) made them earls of Buccleuch.

MODERN SCOTT TARTAN

MODERN BLACK AND WHITE SCOTT TARTAN

Scrymgeour

• The tartan shown was displayed at a gathering of Scrymgeours held at Dudhope Castle, Dundee, in 1971.

• Designed by Donald C. Stewart in 1970, this sett was later adopted as the clan's official tartan.

The name Scrymgeour may derive from the nickname 'Skirmisher' or from *escrimeur*, the French for swordsman. Either way, the name reflects bravery in war. The first to acquire it for valour in battle was Alexander Carron, Royal Standard Bearer of Scotland. His descendant, Alexander Scrymgeour, supported both William Wallace, who granted him lands in Angus, and Robert the Bruce. He was captured by the English in 1306 and hanged. The post of Royal Standard Bearer was hereditary and dangerous: several chiefs of the Clan Scrymgeour were killed in battle while bearing the banner.

ANCIENT SCRYMGEOUR TARTAN

Seton

MODERN SETON TARTAN

• The 'modern' Seton tartan was first recorded in *Vestiarium Scoticum* in 1842.

• This tartan shown, bottom right, is the Seton hunting tartan.

The Clan Seton, originally Norman, secured their family fortunes when Sir Christopher Seton, married a sister of Robert the Bruce and then saved his brother-in-law's life at the battle of Methven in 1306. Seton was taken prisoner and was afterwards executed in London. The Setons had to confront many more family tragedies: the execution of Sir Alexander Seton, Governor of Berwick, in 1333, the deaths of his sons in battle, and the death of George, 3rd Lord Seton at Flodden in 1513. The Setons, who became earls of Winton in 1600, and of Dumfermline in 1606, supported the Stewart cause, but as a result were forced to forfeit their titles.

MODERN SETON HUNTING TARTAN

Shaw

• The Clan Shaw tartan of 1845 was a mistake, the result of errors that occurred in illustrating the Black Watch tartan.

• The tartan was redesigned around 1971 to reflect the clan's Mackintosh and Chattan connections.

The Highland and Lowland Shaws have different origins. The Lowlanders, descendants of William de Shaw, take their name from the Anglo Saxon word scaga, meaning copse; the Highlanders, from an old Gaelic name, Shaeagh or Sithec: Shaw is the anglicized version. Shaw MacDuff, ancestor of the Highland Shaws, also founded the Clan Mackintosh. The Shaws of Tordarroch in Straithnairn were descendants of a 15th-century Mackintosh. Via the Mackintoshes, the Shaws were part of the Clan Chattan federation. After the Shaw lands in Rothiemurchus were sold to Clan Grant in 1567, Clan Chattan tried unsuccessfullyto get them back. Finally, disaster for the Shaws of Rothiemurchus meant a rise for the Shaws of Tordarroch, who were named as chiefs of the name.

MODERN SHAW TARTAN

ANCIENT SHAW OF TORDARROCH TARTAN

Sinclair

• The Sinclair tartan was first recorded in 1831.

• The tartan shown, top right, was worn in a painting by Alexander Sinclair, 13th Earl of Caithness (1790-1858).

The hamlet of St.-Clair-sur-Elle from which the Clan Sinclair took its name reflects their Norman origins. Walderne de Sancto Claro (or St. Clair) came to England at the time of the Norman conquest of 1066, and eventually his descendants settled in Scotland. One of them, Sir William Sinclair became sheriff of Edinburgh and in 1280, acquired the barony of Roslin. In the 14th century, the clan also gained the earldom of Orkney and the Faroe Islands. The Earldom of Caithness followed in 1455, although the Campbells counter-claimed and the Sinclairs' right to Caithness was not finally settled until 1681.

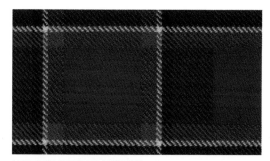

MODERN SINCLAIR TARTAN

MODERN SINCLAIR HUNTING TARTAN

173

Smith/Gow/ MacGowan

• The Smith tartan also can be called the Gow or MacGowan tartan.

• In Gaelic, *gobhan* means 'smith' or 'blacksmith'.

The role of the smith, for fashioning armour, weapons or implements of all sorts, such as iron shoes for horses, was an essential one for all clans, This may explain why the Smith's had numerous connections with other clans. They became known as septs of both the MacPherson and the Mackintosh clans, and through Mackintosh, with the Clan Chattan confederation.

The name 'Smith' appeared in the records in 1199, when Robert the Smith witnessed a charter. In 1274, William the Smith was a member of a jury at an inquest, and in the 14th century a clan named MacGowan was described living by the River Nith on the Borders.

ANCIENT SMITH TARTAN

Stewart

• **This is the clan of the royal house of Scotland (see the Royal Stewart tartans).**

• **The Stewart of Appin sett (bottom right), first known in 1820, is thought to belong to the Mackintosh group of tartans.**

MODERN STEWART TARTAN

The Stewarts, who ultimately became the Scots royal family, had Norman origins. The clan name came from the office of High Steward to King David I, which was given in the 12th century. The High Stewardship of Scotland was later made hereditary by King Malcolm IV. The route to royal status and the adoption of the surname Stewart came after Walter, the 6th High Steward, married the daughter of Robert the Bruce; their son became the first Stewart monarch of Scotland, Robert II, in 1371. However, many Stewart kings would constantly struggle with the recalcitrant Scots nobles and several of them were murdered, died in battle or suffered exile. The Stewarts of Appin were descended from Sir John Stewart of Bonkyl, a son of Alexander, 4th High Steward of Scotland.

STEWART HUNTING TARTAN

MODERN STEWART OF APPIN HUNTING TARTAN

Stuart of Bute

• This maroon background to the Stuart of Bute tartan may be unofficially changed to red in some illustrations.

• The Stuarts of Bute trace their descent from a natural son of Robert II, the first king of the Royal Stewart dynasty.

The ancestral estates of this branch of the royal Stewart family were at Bute, Arran and Cumbrae. The Bute family spell the royal name differently due to a change made while Mary, Queen of Scots was married to the French King Francis II between 1558 and 1560. The change was a concession to the French, whose alphabet does not include the letter 'w' and expresses 'wa' in English and 'oua'. Consequently, 'Stuart' was substituted for 'Stewart' and became the more common spelling for the royal surname.

MODERN STEWART OF BUTE TARTAN

Sutherland

• The tartan show, right, is the 'Old Sutherland', recorded in the *Vestiarium Scoticum* in 1842. The 'New Sutherland' is the same as the Black Watch.

• Sutherland comes from 'Sunderland', which means 'south land', although the surname comes from the Highlands of Scotland.

'South land' describes the southernmost extent of territory owned by the Norse kings of Norway, who ruled the Western Isles until 1266, when they were annexed to the Scots crown. Clan Sutherland is thought to descend from Freskin, a Flemish adventurer in Norman employ who was also the progenitor of the Clan Murray. Hugh, Freskin's grandson, received a grant of land in Morayshire in around 1130 and Freskin's great-grandson, William, was made Earl of Sutherland around 1228. The earldom is thought to be the oldest in Britain.

'OLD SUTHERLAND' TARTAN

Taylor

• The name Taylor is French in origin, deriving from the French verb *tailler*, meaning 'to cut'.

• One version of the name was Cissor, taken from the tailor's most frequently used implement, but this eventually died out.

The Taylors rose to prominence early. Alexander le Taillur may have only been a valet to King Alexander III, but after 1249 there were six landowners named Taylor, all sufficiently important within less than 50 years to be required to sign the Ragman Rolls. The Taylor lands were extensive, including territory in Roxburghshire, Edinburgh, Lanark and the county of Angus in the far north. In the Gaelic-speaking Highlands, the name became Macantaillear, Macintaylor or Macintaileour. In 1613, several Macintaileours sheltered members of the outlawed MacGregor clan and were heavily fined for it.

ANCIENT TAYLOR TARTAN

Turnbull

MODERN TURNBULL DRESS TARTAN

• The unusual Turnbull dress tartan, shown top right, contains no white colouring.

• The more conventional Turnbull hunting tartan is shown bottom right.

The Clan Turnbull owned extensive lands, at Philiphaugh and Hundleshope in border country. Traditionally, the name Turnball goes back to the name given to William Rule, who was said to have saved Robert the Bruce from a goring by 'turning' a charging bull. Later, before the battle of Halidon Hill in 1333, the massively muscled William Turnbull reputedly challenged any Englishman to single combat. Sir Robert Benhale of Norfolk took up the challenge and killed Turnbull's equally hefty mastiff with one blow. He then severed the clansman's left arm and head. Afterwards, the English won the battle.

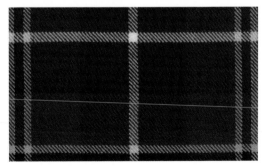

MODERN TURNBULL HUNTING TARTAN

179

Urquhart

• The Urquhart tartan was registered with the Lord Lyon's office in Edinburgh in 1991, although it was first recorded after 1810.

• The origin of the name Urquhart is airchart, meaning rowan wood.

The Urquharts settled in Cromarty in the 14th century. They became hereditary sheriffs and were also constables of the castle in Loch Ness, to which they gave their name.

Canny marriages increased the Urquharts' influence. In the early 14th century, William Urquhart married a daughter of Hugh, Earl of Ross. Two centuries later, Sir Thomas Urquhart of Cromarty married Helen, daughter of Lord Abernethy and then, reputedly, fathered 25 sons. The eldest, Alexander, was granted lands in Ross-shire and Inverness-shire by King James V.

ANCIENT URQUHART TARTAN

Wallace

• The Wallace clan tartan was first recorded in 1842, in the *Vestiarium Scoticum*.

• This tartan (top right) is classed by the Scottish Tartans Society as the Wallace hunting tartan.

Waleis or Wallensis, which became the name Wallace, meant 'foreign', but in Scotland it indicated the name of an ancient Briton who lived in Strathclyde. The Wallaces were first identified as landholders in Ayrshire in the 12th century. Later Wallace branches included the Wallaces of Craigie, Cessnock, Kelly and Cairnhill and the Elderslies. After Malcolm of Elderslie refused to signify alliegance to King Edward I in 1296, he and his eldest son were executed. Malcolm's younger son was William Wallace, the famous Scots freedom fighter. Wallace proved a formidable opponent for the English army, which he defeated at Stirling Bridge in 1297. He was forced to escape to France, but returned in 1303. Two years later he was arrested near Glasgow and was taken to London to suffer the gruesome death accorded traitors – hanging, drawing and quartering.

ANCIENT WALLACE HUNTING TARTAN

WEATHERED WALLACE TARTAN

Weir

• This tartan is listed as the Hope Vere/Weir tartan in the Highland Society Collection.

• The Weir family, were Normans, who originally came from Vere in the Calvados region of France.

The Weirs arrived in Scotland before the battle of Alnwick in 1174. At Alnwick, in which King William the Lion was captured, one Radulphus de Ver was also among the prisoners. At around this time, Radalphus gave land at Spourston in Roxburghshire to the Abbey of Kelso, and one branch of the family, the Weirs of Lesmanhagow, were subsequently vassals of the abbots there. Radulphus' brother, Robert de Ver, is said to have been the progenitor of the Weirs of Blackwood; however, their ancestry can be authenticated only from the year 1400, from the documents containing their acquisition of lands.

MODERN WEIR TARTAN

Wemyss

• The Wemyss clan tartan was first recorded in the *Vestiarium Scoticum* of 1842.

• Wemyss means 'cave' and probably originates from the caves beneath MacDuff Castle.

The Wemyss clan is probably a branch of the MacDuffs, the ancient Earls of Fife. It is therefore one of the few Lowland families who can claim direct descent from ancient Celtic nobility. In 1296, Sir Michael Wemyss swore fealty to the English King Edward I, but later supported Robert the Bruce. Subsequently, the English attacked and pillaged Wemyss Castle. In 1315, after the Bruce's success, this same Sir Michael was one of the witnesses who signed the Act of Settlement of the Scots crown. His son, Sir David Wemyss, placed his seal on the Declaration of Arbroath, which asserted Scots independence in 1320.

ANCIENT WEMYSS TARTAN

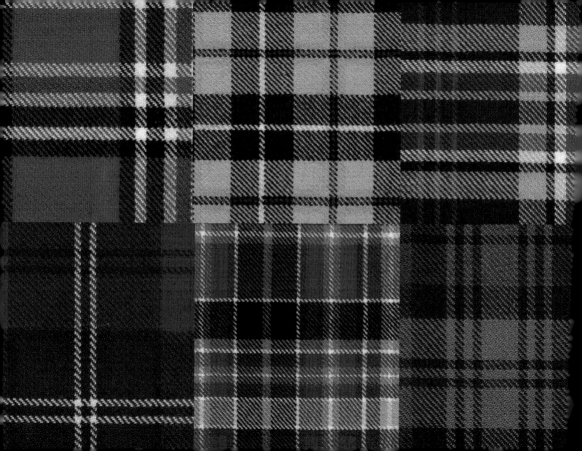

District & Special Tartans

The early district tartans of Scotland, many of which feature in this section, were often precursors of the better known, more numerous, clan tartans. More recently, many new tartans have been designed to celebrate districts or towns such as Aberdeen or Edinburgh, in much the same way as local flags and mascots. Other tartans have been created to commemorate special events, such as the battles of Stirling and Bannockburn.

Also included in this section are the royal tartans created for members of the present Royal Family. Special royal tartans have been produced for three generations of 20th-century royals – King George VI, his daughters Queen Elizabeth II and Princess Margaret, and King Charles III.

Aberdeen

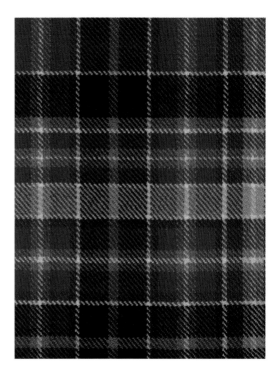

• The Aberdeen is one of the oldest Scots district tartans.

• The first record of the tartan dates back some two centuries.

The first order for an Aberdeen tartan was recorded in the order books of Wilson's of Bannockburn in 1794. The date was significant. The tartan was very old, and most probably, the design had been well known in Scotland for some time. However, after the second Jacobite rebellion of 1745, clan tartans were proscribed, and weavers feared fines and punishments if they made the banned patterns. It seems likely, though, that the Aberdeen was not a tartan to be worn: its design has been considered too large for that purpose, and it is more likely that it was used for blankets, shawls and other larger items.

Angus

• The Angus tartan has a double purpose, serving as both a clan and a district tartan.

• The Clan Angus is probably Celtic in origin.

Situated in eastern Scotland, Angus has a very special place in Scots history: within its borders lies Arbroath, where the famous Declaration of 1320 was signed by the nobles, proclaiming Scotland's independence from England. The Clan Angus took its name from a popular Celtic personal name, Oenghus, which was later anglicized to Angus. The Oenghus who was the traditional progenitor of the clan Angus, was said to be one of those Irish emigrants who crossed to Scotland and founded the kingdom of Dalriada some time in the 5th century. Subsequently, Angus was one of seven sub-kingdoms governed by a mormaer, or local ruler.

ANCIENT ANGUS TARTAN

MODERN ANGUS TARTAN

Black Watch

• In 18th century parlance, a 'watch' meant a military police force.

• The tartan's muted colours earned the regiment that wears it the name Black Watch.

The Black Watch, arguably the most famous of Scots tartans, was designed in 1740 for the Highland regiment of the same name. This regiment was in fact a fusion of six independent militias that were formed between 1725 and 1729. It has been suggested that the tartan's design combined the tartans of the original company captains or of the districts where the original recruitments took place. The regiment's aim was to suppress lawlessness in the Highlands, in particular, cattle stealing, which was known as 'the black trade'. The regiment was at first designated the 43rd; this was changed in 1749 to the 42nd. However, the regiment did not acquire its official name until as recently as 1934. The Black Watch regiment's unequivocal motto *Nemo me impune lacessit* means: 'No one attacks me with impunity'.

ANCIENT BLACK WATCH DRESS TARTAN

MODERN BLACK WATCH TARTAN

Caledonia

• The Caledonia tartan was first recorded in 1819.

• Wilson's of Bannockburn also described the tartan as 'Lovat or Fraser'.

The Caledonia tartan has a romantic name, recalling the time when the Caledonian tribes of Scotland were fierce and free, and even the Roman army feared them. The Romans, who invaded England in 43AD and reached the border with Scotland some 30 years later, considered the Caledonii as the most savage of the British tribes. Nonetheless, they overcame the Caledonii at the battle of Mons Graupius in 84AD and, legend has it, killed 10,000 of them. They had no intention of remaining in Scotland, however, and later built two defences –Hadrian's Wall and the Antonine Wall – to keep the Caledonians out of their province of Britannia.

MODERN CALEDONIA TARTAN

Clergy

• The Scots clergy, which had their own military-style tartan, had to be able to defend themselves, their churches and their congregations.

• In the 18th century, a priest on the island of Skye went to church with a two handled sword, his bow and his arrows.

Where most clansmen owed loyalty to their clans, the Scots clergy also owed obedience to the church. This tartan represents these ties. Considering the ferocity of some clansmen, the Scots clergy did need to defend themselves. A group of MacDonalds once attempted to keep a minister, Colin Campbell, out of his own church at Kilchoan, He came out wearing a kilt – a declaration of war in the circumstances – and armed with a sword and a cocked pistol. Campbell stood firm and saw off his attackers.

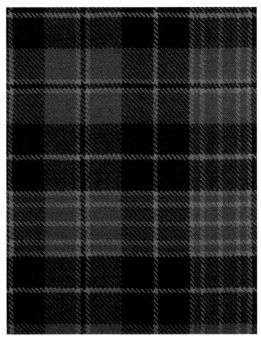

ANCIENT CLERGY TARTAN

Cornish

- Cornwall has always been a vigorously Celtic part of southern England.

- The county can boast no less than five different tartans.

Cornwall was once part of the kingdom of Dumnonia, linked to Celtic areas in Ireland, Wales and Britanny (in northwest France). Its language, Kernewek, is related to Welsh and Breton. The Dumnonian capital, Tintagel, indicates the area's connections with the great Celtic hero 'King' Arthur. Cornwall's five tartans are the Cornish National, Cornish flag, Cornish Hunting, St. Piran Dress and the tartan for Cornish National Day, which was designed in 1963 by the poet E.E. Morton-Nance, who believed that all Celtic peoples, not just the Scots, should consider the tartan as their heritage.

Dunblane

• The Dunblane tartans is one of the rare pre-Culloden tartans.

• In 1822, the Dunblane pattern was re-woven for use during the state visit to Scotland of King George IV.

The Dunblane tartan, which comes from the town of that name in Perthshire, is one of the few that can be authenticated from contemporary evidence. Historians seeking evidence for the designs of early tartans had a piece of good fortune when a portrait at Hornby Castle in Yorkshire came to their attention. In it, Sir Peregrine Hyde Osborne, the 3rd Duke of Leeds and 2nd Viscount Dunblane, is shown wearing a tartan with the pattern illustrated here. Viscount Dunblane, who was born in 1691, died in 1729, soon after succeeding to his titles.

MODERN DUNBLANE TARTAN

Dundee

• The Dundee tartan was recorded in the Wilson's of Bannockburn pattern book of 1819.

• The legendary Kenneth MacAlpin is said to have used Dunblane as a base for his forays against the Picts.

The Dundee sett represents the district tartan for the town of that name, which stands on an ancient site by the River Tay. Traces of Roman military camps, dating from before the 2nd century, have been found in the vicinity. Although recorded in 1819, the Dundee tartan may date from the mid-18th century. The evidence for this can be found in a tartan jacket that was said to have been worn by Bonnie Prince Charlie at the battle of Culloden in 1746. The patterns of the prince's jacket and the tartan have strong similarities.

'OLD DUNDEE' TARTAN

Edinburgh

• The Edinburgh tartan was specially designed for the 9th British Commonwealth Games held in Edinburgh in 1970.

• The tartan's designer, Hugh McPherson, used the colours of the city's coat of arms and those of its football teams.

This was the last Games to be described as 'British Commonwealth': in 1974, they became, simply, the Commonwealth Games and have remained so ever since. However, this 'last' was accompanied by some important firsts: Queen Elizabeth II attended the Games as Head of the Commonwealth for the first time, and the metric system was introduced. It was the largest Games in the history of the event, which first took place in 1930: a record 42 nations and 1700 competitors and officials took part.

Flower of Scotland

• The Flower of Scotland tartan was specially designed and woven as a posthumous tribute to Roy Williamson.

• Williamson, performer with the popular Scots singing group the Corries, died in 1990.

Williamson wrote Flower of Scotland, which became the unofficial Scots anthem. It celebrates the 'flower' of young Scots warriors who died for Robert the Bruce in the early 14th century and defeated English efforts to deprive them of their independence.

'O flower of Scotland,
When will we see your like again
That fought and died for your wee bit
    hill and glen
And stood against him
Proud Edward's army
And sent him homeward tae think again...'

Galloway

• The Galloway is an example of a dual-purpose tartan, used for both clan and district purposes.

• The Galloway tartan was designed in 1950.

The tartan's designer, London chiropodist John Hannay, belonged to an ancient Celtic clan thought to have originated in Galloway. Anyone called Galloway is permitted to wear this tartan. As a surname, Galloway goes back to around 1230, when there is a record of the Abbey of Neubotle receiving land from a certain Thomas de Galwethia. The name Galloway reflects the proximity of 'aliens' in this area of southwestern Scotland, close by the border with England: it comes from the Gaelic word gall, meaning foreigner, though it applied not only to the English, but also to the Scandinavian Vikings and even the Scots Lowlanders.

GALLOWAY HUNTING TARTAN

Glasgow

• **This Glasgow district tartan is one of nine tartans dedicated to this Lanarkshire city.**

• **Glasgow is the largest city in Scotland and the third largest in the United Kingdom.**

The oldest of the Glasgow tartans dates from 1819, and was produced by Wilson's of Bannockburn. Another Glasgow tartan, the 'Rock and Wheel', commemorates an old method of tartan manufacture. More recently, Glasgow Caledonian University has acquired its own tartan, as has the Glasgow Academy, whose sett is based on the Black Watch and celebrates the Academy's merger with the Westbourne School for Girls. The Celtic Society also has its own tartan. A special commemorative sett was produced to commemorate Glasgow '88, 1988 being the year when the Glasgow Garden Festival was held.

Holyrood

• This tartan was initially produced for the celebrations of the Silver Jubilee of Queen Elizabeth II in 1977.

• The design was not initally called Holyrood and, in fact, failed to win royal approval.

The manufacturers, Locharron Weavers, operating on the *nil desperandum* principle, decided to rename the tartan Holyrood, after the Palace of Holyroodhouse in Edinburgh, the Queen's official residence in Scotland. It was an astute move. Holyroodhouse is a key Edinburgh tourist attraction, with thousands of visitors arriving each year to savour the setting of some of Scotland's darkest and most dramatic history. The Holyrood tartan on display has therefore been seen by more people than would otherwise have been the case.

Huntly

• District tartans may have originated with the designs of local weavers. Later, some of these evolved into clan tartans.

• One of these more specialized 'evolved' tartans seems to have been the Huntly district tartan.

Huntly lies in Strathbogie, Aberdeenshire. Huntly Castle was known as Strathbogie Castle until 1314, when Robert the Bruce gave Adam Gordon of Huntly lands in the area. The district tartan, first illustrated in 1893, is thought to have existed in 1745, during the second Jacobite Rebellion, when it was said to have been worn by Bonnie Prince Charlie.

The tartan also made an appearance at Culloden, the battle which ended the Prince's ambitions: it was worn by the Clans Brodie, Forbes, Gordon, MacRae, Munro and Ross.

MODERN HUNTLY TARTAN

Inverness

• Inverness was once the stronghold of the Picts and the site of an imposing royal castle dating from the 12th century.

• The tartan connections of Inverness are Hanoverian and date from around 1822.

The largest town in the northern part of Scotland, with an intimate charm all its own, Inverness has long been regarded as the capital of the Highlands. The Inverness tartan of 1822 was woven for Augustus, the sixth son of King George III, who was created Earl of Inverness, Duke of Susssex and Baron Arklow in 1801. The Inverness is a personal tartan twice over: the same pattern was used for the Princess Elizabeth tartan created in the 1930s. It also doubles as the Burgh of Inverness tartan, one of six that bear this name.

MODERN INVERNESS TARTAN

Irish National tartan

- The Irish National is a modern trade tartan.

- This tartan uses the characteristic 'Irish' emerald colour and is based on a design by Jo Nisbet of Piper's Cove, New Jersey, USA.

Although several 'local' Irish tartans have surfaced in recent times, and there are strong historical and cultural links between the Irish and the Scots, expert opinion is divided as to whether or not the Irish adopted a tartan system. The earliest evidence that they did so comes from a pair of tartan trews dug up with other articles of clothing by an Ulster farmer in 1956; these items dated from the turn of the 17th century. Much later, in 1880, a Paris publisher, J. Claude Fresklie, published Clans Originaux (Original Clans), in which the earliest known records of several Irish tartans were illustrated.

Jacobite

• The Jacobite supporters of the deposed King James VII (of Scotland) and II (of England and Ireland) took their name from Jacobus, the Latin form of James.

• James came to the throne in 1685, intending to restore his kingdom to Roman Catholicism.

Parliament refused to countenance a Catholic renaissance and forced James into exile. Attempts were made to restore the Stewart monarchy in 1689/1690, and in the famous Jacobite rebellions of 1715 and 1745. All failed. More peaceful but no less motivated resistance took place in 1707, when Lowlanders signalled their dislike of the Union of England and Scotland by wearing tartan items. One of these was a tartan silk scarf, which was later used as the basis for the pattern of the Jacobite tartan.

MODERN JACOBITE TARTAN

Lennox

• The Lennox tartan is a district tartan.

• The earliest source for this tartan was Old and Rare Scottish Tartans by D.W. Stewart, which was published in 1893.

Lennox is a long-established Scots family name. Clan-wise, families surnamed Lennox are usually considered relations of the Stewarts or MacFarlanes and some have chosen to wear the ancient Lennox tartan. Coincidentally, the earldom of Lennox was closely connected with the Stewarts, several of whom held the title. Undoubtedly the most famous was the ill-fated Henry Stewart, Lord Darnley, the son of the 4th Earl of Lennox, who married Mary, Queen of Scots and was later murdered. In 1581, Esmé Stuart, who was probably a son of John, the 3rd Earl of Lennox, was created 1st Duke of Lennox.

MODERN LENNOX TARTAN

203

Lorne

• The Lorne tartan was created in 1871 to commemorate a royal marriage.

• The couple were John Douglas Sutherland Campbell, Marquis of Lorne, later 9th Duke of Lorne and Queen Victoria's fourth daughter, Princess Louise.

The tartan, which later became a district tartan, has colours similar to those of the Clan Campbell. The name Lorne came from Loarn, one of the co-founders of the Celtic Kingdom of Dalriada. The Marquis was a commoner, and though Queen Victoria approved of Louise's choice, some of her other children did not want a marriage out of the royal class. The Marquis reminded them that his ancestors had been kings when theirs – the Hanoverians – had been petty rulers in Germany.

ANCIENT LORNE TARTAN

Mar

• The accuracy of the Mar district tartan is disputed, although it has been recorded by the Lord Lyon.

• Mar was one of the ancient Celtic provinces of Scotland and was originally governed by a mormaer, or local ruler.

The mormaers were later designated earls. The first Earl of Moray, Rothri, was mentioned in a document dated 1114. In around 1295, Isabella of Mar married Robert the Bruce, so forging a connection between the 'tribe of Mar' and the future royal family of Scotland. The tartan's designer is not known, but it may date from before 1850. The tartan has been named as belonging to the Clan Skene, a family that lived in the Mar district, together with the Robertsons, though this naming is controversial.

MODERN MAR TARTAN

Paisley

• The Paisley tartan is modern, created in 1952 by Allan C. Drennan, an assistant manager in one of the town's department stores.

• Drennan's design, which he considered bore 'a motif of the Clan Donald', was a great success, winning first prize in the Highland Show at Kelso.

The designer's intention was to create a district tartan for Paisley, which is situated in Renfrewshire, a few kilometres from Glasgow, and is less well known for its tartans than for its famous shawls and other textiles. However, Drennan's prize-winning success brought his design to the attention of families bearing the old Scots and Irish surname of Paisley, and they took it up as a personal tartan. The tartan also became the 'official' tartan of the Paisley and Allied Families Society.

ANCIENT PAISLEY TARTAN

Royal tartans

• The Royal Stewart tartan (top right) can only be worn by members of the British royal family.

• The Prince of Wales tartan (centre right) features colours reminiscent of the green, red and white of the Welsh flag.

MODERN ROYAL STEWART TARTAN

This tartan once belonged to the monarchs of the House of Stewart. The Stewart dynasty comprised the five kings and two queens regnant who occupied the thrones of Scotland, England and Ireland between 1603 and 1714. However, there are no less than 69 Stewart tartans in the archives of the Scottish Tartans Society, 37 of which are classed as clan tartans, another five as dress tartans and seven as hunting tartans. The Balmoral tartan is still exclusive to the Royal Family. The choice of tartans that the Prince of Wales wears is governed by the occasion. When he visits Scotland, he can wear the tartan of Lord of the Isles, one of the many titles he holds. Another of the Prince's titles is Duke of Rothesay, and he wears the hunting variant of the Rothesay tartan.

MODERN PRINCE OF WALES TARTAN

ANCIENT DUKE OF ROTHESAY HUNTING TARTAN

Stirling and Bannockburn

• The Stirling and Bannockburn tartan dates from around 1847.

• It commemorates two great Scots victories.

Both triumphs came in the fight for independence from England. In the first, in 1297, the clans led by William Wallace crushed the Earl of Surrey's army at Stirling Bridge, so provoking the English King Edward I to invade Scotland in 1298. Seventeen years later, at Bannockburn, Robert the Bruce thrashed a numerically superior army led by King Edward II. The tartan is relatively recent, dating from around 1847, when it was introduced by Wilson's of Bannockburn for the Stirling and Bannockburn Caledonian Society. The tartan presently available is a modernized version, rewoven by the tartan expert John Cargill of Dundee.

Tweedside

• The Tweedside, one of the older district tartans, dates from around 1840.

• The first record of the tartan appears in the pattern book of Wilson's of Bannockburn.

The Tweedside tartan comes from the area around the River Tweed, on the border between Scotland and England. The predominance of red in the design seems only too appropriate, since Tweedside witnessed some of the bloodiest encounters in the long rivalry between the English and the Scots.

Equally, the Tweedside area, with its many natural beauties, has also inspired some of the finest Scots literature. Most Border ballads, for example, had a Tweedside setting and the novelist Sir Walter Scott found inspiration here after he settled at Abbotsford, on the banks of the River Tweed.

MODERN TWEEDSIDE TARTAN

209

Canadian Tartans

Canada, a country built on immigration, owes a great deal to the Scots settlers, the first of whom arrived in Nova Scotia – New Scotland – after 1621. As more settlers established themselves in Cape Breton and beyond in the 17th century, Canada acquired, and has retained, a strong Scots ambience. Many more families were driven from their country by the brutal Highland Clearances of 1763–76 and took with them local traditions, including the making and wearing of tartans.

The tartan has since become much more than a garment peculiar to the Scots. As the emigrants and their descendents settled in Canada new types of tartan design developed. The tartan itself was a symbol of the 'old' country, but the features and colours of the 'new' country provided new, distinctively Canadian patterns.

Alberta

• The Alberta tartan was devised in 1961.

• The designers were two women living and working in Edmonton, capital of the westernmost of Canada's three 'prairie' provinces.

The idea of designing a special tartan arose from the activities of the Edmonton Rehabilitation Society, a charitable agency which taught disabled students useful skills ito improve their work prospects. One such skill was using handlooms to weave textiles. The special tartan – which provided welcome publicity for the Society – was developed by Alison Lamb, director of the Society, and Ellen Neilsen, the Society's weaving instructor. Their project succeeded beyond all expectation. The Alberta tartan not only promoted the work of the Society, it also became the official district tartan of the province.

British Columbia

• The British Columbia tartan was designed by Eric Ward and manufactured by Pik Mills of Quebec.

• The tartan was created in 1966.

British Columbia, the most westerly of the Canadian provinces, lies on the west coast, and in the 18th century its coastline was visited by intrepid navigators, including Captain James Cook during his explorations of the Pacific. Alexander Mackenzie, a Scot from Stornaway, probed the interior of what later became the province of British Columbia, which was established as a Crown Colony of the British Empire in 1858. In 1866, the governments of British Columbia and Vancouver Island merged and a century later, this tartan was designed to commemorate the event.

Canada Maple Leaf

• In 1965, when a new Canadian flag was devised, the maple leaf was a natural choice for the basis of its design.

• The new flag was commemorated by a special tartan featuring the brilliant red, brown and green of the maple's autumn foliage.

Canada and the maple tree are virtually synonymous. The maple's spectacular foliage and colouring have made its leaf the country's national symbol. The maple is also the basis of a profitable business. After Europeans settled in Canada in the 17th and 18th centuries, they learned how to tap the trunk of the maple tree to extract the sap, which had been used for centuries to sweeten native American dishes. Today, the syrup distilled from this sap is worth more than C$100 millions (£44.6 million) a year.

Cape Breton

• In 1629, Scots founded one of the first settlements on Cape Breton Island, Nova Scotia.

• Cape Breton Island officially acquired that most distinctive symbol of Scotland, a tartan, in 1957.

The Cape Breton settlers brought Scots culture to the New World, and it has influenced this eastern area of Canada ever since. The tartan was designed by Elizabeth Grant, to a colour scheme from a poem by Lillian Crewe Walsh, written in 1907:

'Grey for our Cape Breton Steel
Gold for the golden sunsets shining bright on
    the lakes of Bras D'Or
Green for our lofty mountains, our valleys and
    our fields
To show us God's hand has lingered
To Bless Cape Breton's shore.'

Manitoba

• Manitoba's tartan comes with two slightly different variations.

• The original pattern was designed in 1962 by Hugh Kirkwood Rankine.

Manitoba's history is woven into the tartan. In 1812, crofters from the Scots Highlands founded the Red River Settlement, which was the site of a rebellion in 1869 by French-speaking settlers, who had been ignored when the Hudson's Bay Company sold its land rights to the new Dominion of Canada. The Red River Settlement accounts for the red in the tartan design, and later grew into Manitoba's largest city, Winnipeg. The blue lines in the Manitoba tartan were taken from the Clan Douglas tartan and commemorated Thomas Douglas, 5th Earl of Selkirk, who promoted the Settlement.

New Brunswick

• New Brunswick is situated close to the Gulf of St. Lawrence in eastern Canada.

• Its name honours the Hanoverian dynasty, descended from the family of Brunswick-Lènebur.

The Hanoverians became monarchs of Scotland, England and Ireland in 1714, more than 90 years after Scots first settled in Canada.

The tartan was commissioned in 1959 by William Aitken, Lord Beaverbrook (1879–1964). A Scots-Canadian born in Maple, Ontario, he came to Britain in 1910, and soon entered politics. During World War II, he was minister of aircraft production. He also became a newspaper proprietor. The New Brunswick tartan was designed by Loomcrofters of Fredericton, the provincial capital, and its colours included 'beaver brown' in Beaverbrook's honour.

Newfoundland

• Newfoundland, an island in the Gulf of St. Lawrence, was discovered by John and Sebastian Cabot in 1497.

• The province was the last to join the Canadian federation, in 1949.

Designed in 1972 by Louis Anderson, the tartan reflects one of the province's industries, forestry, and *Ode to Newfoundland* explains the yellow and white:

> When Sun-rays crown the pine-clad hills,
> And Summer spreads her hand,
> When silvern voices tune thy rills,
> We love thee, smiling land....
> When spreads thy cloak of shimm'ring white,
> At Winter's stern command,
> Thro' shortened day and starlit night,
> We love thee, frozen land.

Nova Scotia

• The Nova Scotia tartan was designed by Mrs Douglas Murray, President of the Halifax Weavers' Guild.

• She based her design on the blue, white and yellow of the provincial flag.

Nova Scotia – New Scotland – was founded after 1621 by Sir William Alexander, later Earl of Stirling. Unfortunately, the settlement bankrupted him and he died insolvent in 1640. Nova Scotia, however, became a thriving concern, with sheep farming among its many successful industries. At a sheep breeders' convention in 1953, Mrs. Murray displayed a shepherd wearing a kilt as part of a woollen panel designed to illustrate sheep shearing history. The design was so admired that it afterwards became the official tartan of the province.

Ontario

• Like the Plaid du Quebec, the Ontario tartan was based on the province's official coat of arms, awarded by Queen Victoria in 1868.

• The tartan was designed almost a century later, in 1965, by Rotex Ltd.

The colours of the tartan reflect the elements of the province's coat of arms. The three maple leaves are represented by the green background and yellow lines. The cross of St. George is echoed by the red lines. The bear, which is the chief animal featured on the province's crest, accounts for the black in the tartan, and the brown reflects the colours of the moose and deer that serve as supporters on the left and right of the coat of arms.

Ontario's two other tartans are the Ensign of Ontario and a tartan for Northern Ontario.

Prince Edward Island

• Prince Edward Island, the smallest of Canada's ten provinces, lies in the Gulf of St. Lawrence in the east of the country.

• Originally a French colony first claimed in 1603, it was ceded to Britain in 1763, after the French defeat in the Seven Years' War.

The island was originally named Ile St. Jean, or St. John's Island, but was renamed in 1799 in honour of Prince Edward Augustus, son of King George III. The Prince Edward Island tartan, designed in 1964, marked the centenary of an important event in the province's history: in 1864, Charlottetown, capital of Prince Edward Island, was the site for the Canadian Confederation Conference. This organized Canada's provinces into the federal Dominion that became a political reality three years later.

Quebec

• Quebec, Canada's largest province, stands on the mighty St. Lawrence River.

• The province has two tartans.

Quebec was once the colony of New France and the pride of the French empire in America. It was ceded to Britain in 1763, after the French defeat in the Seven Years' War and still retains its Gallic flavour. Of Quebec's two tartans, one is a dress tartan known as the Centennial – meaning the centennial of the Canadian federation in 1967– and the other, shown here, is the Plaid du Quebec, which takes its cue from the province's coat of arms. The blue represents the background on the coat of arms to a trio of fleurs de lys, a famous symbol of France, and the white is for the scroll which contains the motto *Je me souviens* (I remember).

Saskatchewan

• **The central prairie province of Saskatchewan is popularly known as 'Canada's breadbasket'.**

• **The 'breadbasket' identity is reflected in the colouring of the Saskatchewan tartan.**

The tartan was designed in 1961 by Mrs Frank Bastedo, wife of a former Lieutenant Governor of Saskatchewan, which is also the name of the local river and means 'fast flowing' in the native Cree language.

Saskatchewan's most important crops, wheat and rapeseed, and the province's plentiful sunflowers, lend their gold and yellow hues to the tartan. Much of Saskatchewan is covered in coniferous forest, hence the green featured in the tartan. The red represents the Saskatchewan lily; the black squares represent the oil and coal produced in the province.

Yukon

• Yukon's most significant claim to fame was the discovery of gold in the Klondyke River in 1896.

• The subsequent gold 'rush' increased Yukon's population to a record 27,000 by 1901.

Situated in the far northwest of Canada and adjacent to the US state of Alaska, Yukon's topography consists mainly of mountains, including Canada's loftiest peak, Mount Logan. These and other features provide motifs for the Yukon's tartan, designed by Janet Couture in 1965; a major influence was the proximity of the Dominion of Canada's centenary in 1967. The small yellow, nugget-sized squares featured on the tartan represent the gold rush, but there is also purple for the province's mountains, white for its snow-capped peaks and magenta for the colour of the Yukon's floral emblem, fireweed.